Domeliners
Yesterday's Trains of Tomorrow

Karl Zimmermann

KALMBACH BOOKS

Printed in Hong Kong

97 98 99 00 01 02 03 04 05 06   10 9 8 7 6 5 4 3 2 1

For more information, visit our website at
http://www.kalmbach.com

Publisher's Cataloging-in-Publication
(Provided by Quality Books, Inc.)

Zimmermann, Karl R.
   Domeliners : yesterday's trains of tomorrow /
Karl Zimmermann. — 1st ed.
   cm.
   Includes bibliographical references and index.
   ISBN: 0-89024-292-5

   1. Railroads—United States—Passenger cars.
2. Railroads—United States—Trains. I. Title.

TF457.Z56 1997   385'.22'0973
                              QBI97-721

Book and cover design: Kristi Ludwig

Contents

Foreword
The Domeliner Mystique

Half a century ago, a bright, intriguing, even radical idea lit up the traditionally conservative landscape of railroading. The idea was the dome car, and it caught on — to the point that dome cars came to loom large in the perception of North American passenger railroading in its last great years, those immediately following World War II. The charismatic cars would assume an importance far out of proportion to their rather slight numbers. Just 236 were ever built, and the time line for their construction was little more than a decade long. Only 16 railroads bought dome cars from three builders: the Budd Company, Pullman-Standard, and American Car & Foundry. These railroads were the Santa Fe, Baltimore & Ohio, Canadian Pacific, Chesapeake & Ohio, Burlington Route, Milwaukee Road, Rio Grande, Great Northern, Missouri Pacific, Northern Pacific, Southern Pacific, Spokane, Portland & Seattle, Texas & Pacific, Union Pacific, Wabash, and Western Pacific. Southern Pacific and Burlington built their own, in the latter case merely as prototypes. Another handful — principally Illinois Central, Canadian National, Amtrak, Auto-Train, and VIA Rail Canada — operated them as hand-me-downs.

These cars, designed to provide high visibility for passengers, also *had* high visibility. They were exciting, glamorous, and innovative. Seen by many as the possible savior of the passenger train — in the West, at least, where more ample clearances allowed their use — domes did what could be done against long odds. The public, whose freshest image of passenger railroading was dominated by war-swollen consists shorn by law of all nonutilitarian equipment, responded to the lure of domes. Many came back to trains for another look and found the dome cars to be as much fun as the railroad publicists had promised.

This book has been a long time in gestation, and a number of friends have made significant contributions to its progress along the way. In addition to providing invaluable photographs, Bob Schmidt has been unflagging in his research assistance and general support of the project. Bill Howes has opened his extensive collection of memorabilia and photographs, and given generously of his time and effort in so doing. Mike Schafer, a major contributing photographer, has been a collaborator on this project since it began as a pair of articles in *Passenger Train Journal* more than a decade ago. Roger Cook not only provided photographs but also helped in the painful process of winnowing down an overabundance of outstanding illustration. Phil Dohmen shared his encyclopedic knowledge of the current whereabouts of every extant dome. Steve Patterson supplied the book's cover photo (something of a Patterson/Zimmermann tradition over the years) and other photographs as well.

Important photographs, memorabilia, and information have also come through the generosity of Ted Benson, Mike Blaszak, Jim Boyd, Mike Caramanna, Tom Dixon of the Chesapeake & Ohio Historical Society, Mel Finzer, Steve Glischinski, Herbert Harwood, Dave Ingles, John Ingles, Bob Johnston, Dick Kindig, Bill Kratville at the Union Pacific Historical Museum, J. Parker Lamb, Larry Mack, Fred Matthews, Bill Middleton, the Milwaukee Public Library, Bruce Nelson, Howard Patrick, Richard Pegler of Along Different Lines, Gary Schlerf, Jim Scribbins, Bill Taylor, Peter Tilp, Richard Tower, Chard Walker, Joe Welsh, and Doug Wornom.

Others closer to home have helped, too. Catherine Zimmermann, my mother, is an eagle-eyed proofreader and general supporter of these writing enterprises—as is Laurel, my wife. As always, they merit my most special thanks.

— *Karl Zimmermann*

Southern Pacific's full-length dome, carried in the summer of 1969 aboard the *Coast Daylight*, was exceptionally well appointed. (Karl Zimmermann)

Union Pacific's dome diners ran on the *City of Portland* and (shown here) the *City of Los Angeles*.
(Roger Cook)

Famous domes that lasted into the Amtrak era, both home-grown rebuildings: Burlington's "pattern dome"
and Southern Pacific's full-length, low-profile model, caught at Chicago in 1971. The SP dome is on the
westbound *City of San Francisco*. (Mike Schafer)

7

The Pioneers
Silver Dome and the *Train of Tomorrow*

Cyrus R. Osborn, a vice-president of General Motors and general manager of that company's Electro-Motive Division, is the generally acknowledged father of the dome car, and his inspiration is said to have come on July 4, 1944, on Denver & Rio Grande Western's rails through Colorado's Glenwood Canyon. Riding in the cab of a pioneering FT diesel locomotive on an expedition to study

General Motors published an oversized brochure to publicize its *Train of Tomorrow*. (Author's Collection)

General Motors built 10-foot-long models of the *Train of Tomorrow* cars. This is observation Moon Glow. (General Motors: *Trains* Magazine Collection)

wartime freight movements through the Rockies, he was struck by the grandeur of his unobstructed view of mountains and river through the locomotive's expansive, sloped windshield.

"If people knew what they could see from here," Osborn remarked to the engineer, "they would pay $500, just to sit in the fireman's seat from Chicago to the Coast."

Salt Lake City was Osborn's destination on that trip. There, in his room at the Hotel Utah, he made some sketches on hotel stationery of an upper-deck observatory with a ramp leading down to a passenger compartment with a depressed floor. After he got back to his office in LaGrange, Indiana, he confirmed the concept's essential feasibility with EMD's engineering department.

GM was impressed enough with Osborn's idea to bring the project to Harley Earl, vice-president in charge of the Styling Section. Under Earl's direction, staff designers created some 1,500 sketches of dome cars. About one hundred were workable and promising; from these sprang the General Motors *Train of Tomorrow*.

"The next step was a model of a three-car train made of wood, metal, and plastics," Franklin Reck has recorded in *On Time*, EMD's corporate history. "Each car, ten feet long, was populated with tiny clay figures of men, women, and children, seated, standing, or walking about. In the diner, miniature waiters served food. In the highly modern dressing rooms, tiny ladies primped before mirrors. In the glass dome sections, passengers sat, looking out at the painted mountain scenery that formed a backdrop for the model."

Burlington issued a folder touting its experimental Silver Dome. (Author's Collection)

These models and drawings for the *Train of Tomorrow* with its "Astra Liner" domes were displayed in the winter and spring of 1945 to successive groups of high-ranking railroad executives. Officers from more than fifty Class 1 railroads, 19 railroad presidents among them, were reported to have studied the designs. Their suggestions were solicited, and some eventually were incorporated in the demonstration train that was the culmination of GM's project. Powered by an Electro-Motive Division E7, the four-

car, all-Astra-Dome *Train of Tomorrow* would eventually be completed by Pullman-Standard Car Manufacturing Company in May 1947. But these cars missed being the first domes by almost two years.

Among the railroad executives who viewed GM's brainchild on the drawing board at the trade exhibitions, none was more intrigued than Ralph Budd, president of the Chicago, Burlington & Quincy (but no relation to Edward G. Budd, the carbuilder about to enter the dome story). The idea was not new to him. A

10

Silver Dome, the first modern dome car, was created in Burlington's Aurora Shops from coach Silver Alchemy. The unbroken line of windows set it apart from its purpose-built successors. Pre-rollout publicity promoted the increase in seating capacity from 52 to 58, "an important help toward accommodating heavy wartime traffic." This assumed that seats in the dome would be assigned as revenue places, which they turned out not to be. (Chicago, Burlington & Quincy: *Trains* Magazine Collection)

friend of Osborn's, he had been among the first to see sketches of the new concept. "If you think the idea is crazy," Osborn had said, "throw it away and no one will hear of it."

Budd thought it far from crazy. He was sufficiently intrigued to instruct H. H. Ulrich, Burlington's mechanical chief, that a coach then in the road's Aurora, Illinois, shops — No. 4714, Silver Alchemy, which had been delivered by the Edward G. Budd Manufacturing Company in 1940 — should emerge with "something added." Using certain Astra-Liner concepts being developed for the Train of Tomorrow, Col. E. J. Ragsdale of Budd and his staff collaborated with Burlington mechanical engineers. In June of 1945, out rolled Silver Dome, first by far.

Silver Dome proved a great success during testing on various Burlington trains, and within six months Burlington (together with future *California Zephyr* part-

ners Western Pacific and Denver & Rio Grande Western) had placed an order for 40 new domes on the strength of its performance, despite the fact that the car was necessarily makeshift in certain ways. For one thing, though the *Train of Tomorrow* projected curved glass in the dome, manufacturers still geared for the war effort could not deliver it, so the Burlington's dome was squared off, built of flat glass.

For another, though GM's Astra-Liner plans called for a depressed floor under the dome, this proved an impossible modification to an existing car without major frame reconstruction. An expedient if imperfect solution for Silver Dome was to place coach seats lengthwise under the dome — facing out, not forward. Passengers walking through the coach passed between the seats and the widows, under headroom provided by the raised platform beneath seats in the dome. But despite these shortcomings the dome idea was clearly a winner.

11

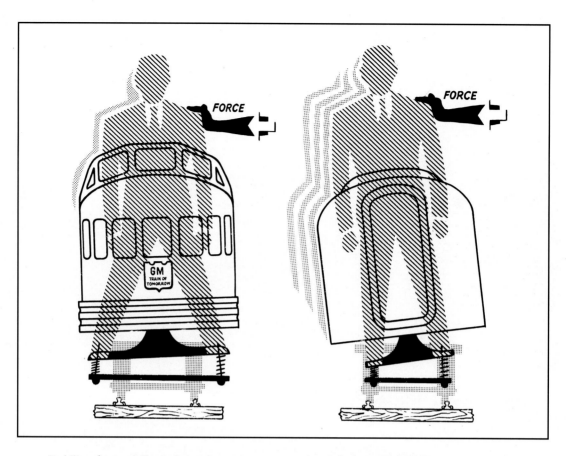

Stability of potentially top-heavy dome cars was a concern right from the beginning. This illustration shows the advantage of outside swing hangers on the trucks used on the *Train of Tomorrow* and other domes. The illustrative analogy: with feet spread wide apart, a person can better resist a shove from the side. (General Motors: *Trains* Magazine Collection)

As built, Silver Alchemy's height was 13 feet 6½ inches from the rail top; Silver Dome would be 16 feet 1½ inches high, still well under the 17-foot 3-inch height of certain freight cars then operating virtually system-wide on the Burlington (but about three inches higher than any production dome would ever be). The dome's vertical extension of 2 feet 7 inches would put passengers head and shoulders above the roof line, providing fine views in all directions, including forward and back along the train. Illumination was arranged so only floor lights had to be kept lit after dark, allowing the magical nighttime vistas by headlight or moonlight that subsequent generations of dome-riders have enjoyed.

Silver Dome had 18 reclining chair seats forward, 24 in the dome, and 16 underneath — 12 in back-to-back pairs separated by a glass partition and facing the windows, and four facing each other across a table suitable for playing cards. This netted a total of 58 seats compared to Silver Alchemy's 52, but 24 of that number were nonrevenue, unreserved dome seats. (The proposition of assigning dome seats at a small supplemental charge was much debated in the planning stages, but Burlington came down definitively on the other side — and subsequent dome operators have almost all followed that lead.) Aboard Silver Dome, luggage storage was provided along the sides of the stairway to the dome, and the women's lounge filled the rear section of the main floor.

By moving rest rooms into the depressed under-dome area, Budd's production dome chair cars for Burlington would offer from 46 to 54 revenue seats on the main floor — a considerable improvement on Silver Dome's 34. This makes all the more curious and puzzling a footnote to the dome-car story. In June 1949, fully four years after Silver Dome's creation and well after a substantial dome fleet had arrived from Budd, Silver Dome received an identical twin. Silver Castle, another "class of 1940" Budd-built chair car in pool service, rolled out of Burlington's Aurora shops with name unchanged — but rebuilt as a Silver Dome clone, with all its experimental awkwardnesses. Meanwhile, GM's project had proceeded apace. And when it finally arrived, the glass-and-steel reality born

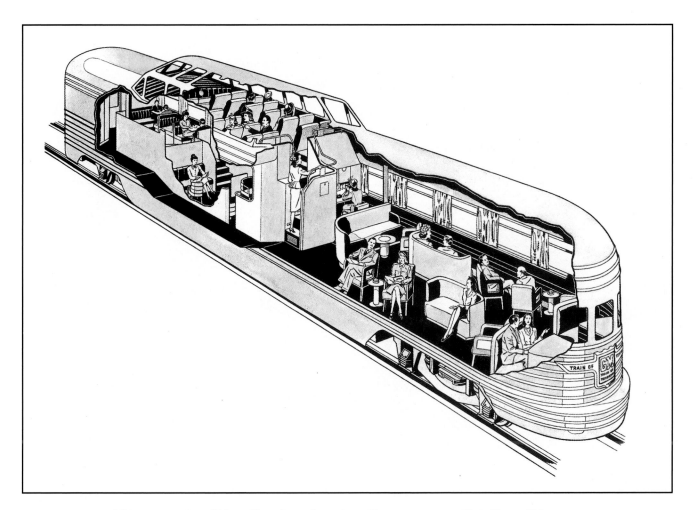

This cutaway view of Moon Glow shows the variety of lounge spaces provided. (General Motors: *Trains* Magazine Collection)

of hundreds and hundreds of plans, drawings, and cogitations, the built-from-scratch *Train of Tomorrow* had easily solved the recessed floor problem, but its domes had glass as flat as Silver Dome's — and so, in fact, would all the early Pullman-Standard domes.

The *Train of Tomorrow* — handsomely dressed in blue and stainless steel when it rolled out of Pullman-Standard's shops and into the public eye on May 28, 1947, at Soldiers' Field in Chicago — was the result of collaboration among P-S designers and engineers, Electro-Motive engineers, and stylists from GM's Detroit plants, who were responsible for the interiors. Its consist was 72-seat chair car Star Dust, dining car Sky View, sleeper Dream Cloud, and observation-lounge Moon Glow. Dream Cloud had eight duplex roomettes, two drawing rooms, and, under the dome, three compartments, each with two lengthwise lower berths. On the point was EMD E7 No. 765, with stainless-steel sheathing on its flanks to match the cars and the name "General Motors" inscribed in the tail of a starburst.

The *Train of Tomorrow* and Silver Dome evolved

very much in tandem, as developmental partners rather than competitors, together defining what would be the broad-brush look of all the dome cars built subsequently. This collaboration was underlined by the Burlington-General Motors decision to couple Silver Dome's first test-demonstration run with the GM announcement of its intention to let contracts for a Train of Tomorrow.

Both took place in Chicago on July 23, 1945. In the consist of CB&Q's No. 45 for Minneapolis, Silver Dome glided out of Union Station at 10 a.m. loaded with Burlington officials and journalists. Meanwhile, Cyrus Osborn was announcing that GM would be contracting with an existing carbuilder — Pullman-Standard, as it would turn out — to construct the *Train of Tomorrow* to designs of GM's creation.

"Our sole purpose is to contribute to the post-war success of American railroads, with which Electro-Motive Division is so closely identified," Osborn said, explaining the seemingly anomalous presence of GM in passenger-car building. "We have taken steps to

General Motors and Pullman-Standard created a variety of new spaces in the *Train of Tomorrow*. Most striking was the dome area of diner *Sky View*; publicists proclaimed a "roof-garden" atmosphere. The main-floor dining room, seen from the stairs to the dome, was attractive too. Observation *Moon Glow*'s under-dome lounge was cozy but lacked windows. (General Motors: *Trains* Magazine Collection.)

protect the designs, but only for the purpose of preventing someone tying them up to restrict usage. We have informed railroads and car-building companies that they may freely use the designs."

When General Motors designers had first begun playing with Osborn's inspiration, some of these concepts and renderings were quite futuristic, defining vehicles that might have been as much at home on the launching pad as on railroad tracks. (Ralph Budd, in revealing Burlington's own Silver Dome plan at an Executive Club luncheon in Chicago in March of 1945, said that *Train of Tomorrow* plans were proceeding "without any inhibitions or restrictions such as past railroad practices or standards.") As finally built, how-

ever, GM's train was advanced but — aside from the dome-car concept — not radical.

Right from the initial announcement GM was at pains to make clear that it had no intention of entering the passenger-car business itself. Still, the corporation's participation in the actual construction of the train would be significant: locomotive by the Electro-Motive Division, air conditioning by the Frigidaire Division, anti-friction journal-box bearings by the Hyatt Bearings Division, and diesel generating equipment by Detroit Diesel Division and Delco Products Division.

"The Astra Liner designs are the work of the General Motors Styling Section at Detroit," Osborn

Proud of bagging the *Train of Tomorrow* contract, Pullman-Standard advertised its conquest widely. In the streamliner era, P-S would all too often come in second to The Budd Company. (Author's Collection)

explained in his July 1945 announcement. "Artists, sculptors, and designers of the Styling Section were given a free hand to suggest improvements in train travel that they themselves would enjoy as passengers."

The design team came up with four then-unique

cars that introduced a slew of new ideas; some were seeds that germinated and reached full flower elsewhere, while others fell on barren ground.

Railway Age reported in detail on the plans. "A reserved seat in the Astra Dome of each sleeping car of the Astra Liner," the magazine said (though it turned out that there would be but one sleeper), "goes with each space in a room on the lower deck." With 24 seats in the dome, and just 20 berths in the car as built, this early attempt at solving what would become a classic dome problem — seat shortage — could have worked.

"This feature," *Railway Age* continued, speaking of the domes, "adds the charm and luxury ordinarily associated with a deck chair on an ocean liner, with the greater attraction that the scenery from a train is much more interesting."

The dome-sleeper eventually delivered by Pullman-Standard as Dream Cloud was slightly different from the GM design announced in July 1945. Carried out as planned were the two three-berth drawing rooms forward and three two-berth compartments under the dome.

The drawing rooms were unique, reached by a lateral passageway between the rooms that tapped off the main corridor, which ran along the left side of the car. There was a door to close off the passageway from the corridor, creating a private en-suite enclave of the two drawing rooms and their shared toilet, which was between the rooms at the end of the short hall. Each drawing room had a long sofa on the inside wall facing the window, plus two loose club chairs. The sofa converted to a lower berth, and two uppers folded out of the walls.

Two of the three under-dome compartments were configured similarly to the drawing rooms for daytime use — a sofa facing the window and two club chairs. The sofa converted to a lower berth, and a second lower folded out of the wall. (As built all three rooms were set up this way, though for a time one of them was to have a fold-up double bed, similar to the arrangement described below.) Toilets and washbasins dropped out of the wall and, at least as projected in the original specifications, a screen could be pulled out to provide some privacy.

Originally the aft end of the car was to have three single bedrooms, a bedroom with a double bed, and a shower and toilet room. In this highly unusual arrangement, the rearmost single, the double, and the shower and toilet could have been combined into a lavish suite.

"By opening a collapsible wall between the two bedrooms," *Railway Age* reported, "a living room almost as large as a small hotel bedroom is attained. Arranged for daytime occupancy, the double bed folds into the wall opposite the window. A small table and two seats unfold from the bottom of the bed, to provide game or writing facilities, or serve as a coffee table.

Two comfortable lounge chairs are placed by the window. Other folding chairs may be brought in by the porter if required."

These would have been the most spacious railroad passenger accommodations ever, outside of a private car. But as it turned out, the suite and single bedrooms never came to pass, since the after end of the car was given over to eight duplex roomettes instead. Ironically, in spite of the considerable study and planning about configuration of berths, they would hardly ever be slept in anyway, since the car would spend its service life as a parlor car. And Pullman-Standard would never build another dome sleeper.

If sleeper Dream Cloud was a lovely one-of-a-kind curiosity, diner Sky View would become the prototype for some of the most wonderful railroad cars ever built: the dome diners that would run on Union Pacific's *City of Portland* and *City of Los Angeles*. No other railroad ever ordered dome diners — and, in fact, the concept almost didn't make it into the *Train of Tomorrow*.

Originally GM's Styling Section had offered two alternate suggestions for the train's dining car. One, domeless, would have retained the car's roof line but with large curved-glass skylights on the shoulders — an arrangement much like what Pullman-Standard executed in 1956 as Sun Lounges for Seaboard Air Line's *Silver Meteor*. Again, though the car was never built, *Railway Age*'s reportage intrigues for the light it sheds on the thinking of the time. The glassed ceiling, the magazine said, "gives the diner the characteristics of a fashionable out-of-doors cafe or roof garden. Two end tables may be removed and folded into slots in the side walls. This leaves an intimate space in which five or six couples may dance after dinner."

Dancing aside, the next generation of train riders should have rejoiced that GM chose the other option — the dome diner. (This must have been a last-minute decision, since early publicity art shows the domeless version.) Original plans called for seating in the dome and in both ends of the car, with the kitchen in the depressed under-dome section.

As built, however, Sky View carried its kitchen on the main floor and seated 18 passengers in the dome, 24 in the main dining room at angled tables (for two on one side of the car and four on the other), and 10 more in a private room under the dome. Food reached waiters in the dome by dumbwaiter. Other than the seating capacity of the main room, this description could apply to UP's ten "City" dome diners as well as the *Train of Tomorrow*.

Moon Glow, the observation car, had four separate sections: a lounge with assorted curved-back sofas and moveable chairs in the rounded observation end; two cocktail lounges, one under the dome and one at the car's forward end; and the dome itself, with the 24 coach-style seats that would prove to be the standard. "The seating may be varied," *Railway Age* conjectured, regarding the dome area and renewing the deck-chair analogy. "It would be possible on transcontinental trains to equip the dome with fewer seats of chaise-longue style for sunbathing or a quiet nap." All told, more than half the car's 68 seats were movable, forming groups "as in clubs, homes and on shipboard."

The car was actually to have had four levels, since the observation-room floor was specified 18 inches above the main-floor level — an attractive feature that Pullman-Standard would later use in observation cars delivered to Southern in 1950 for the *Royal Palm* and the *Crescent*.

Dome coach Star Dust seated 72 passengers, including 24 in the dome. Underneath there were three semiprivate rooms, "ideal for family traveling," according to the *Train of Tomorrow* brochure. At its aft end the dome was open to the main coach level. (Other variations of this under-dome openness, the sometimes surprising absence of the bulkheads that in Budd domes would be structural, would appear in subsequent P-S cars for Baltimore & Ohio and Missouri Pacific.)

The cumulative effect of this four-dome consist on the thousands that toured it must have been magical, so numerous and provocative were the innovations. And in spite of Silver Dome's early appearance on the scene and the fact that 49 Budd domes would be in service before the first order stimulated by the *Train of Tomorrow* was filled by Pullman-Standard, the barnstorming train legitimized this carefully worded claim by the carbuilder's publicists: "Pullman-Standard solved the challenging engineering and construction problems that had to be met in building the first all-new Dome Coach . . . the first Dome Sleeper . . . and the first Dome Diner. . . ."

Even before the Soldiers' Field dedication, the press had gotten a peek at the new train. In February 1947, colored sketches and new materials to be incorporated had been unveiled, and certain unique construction features of the cars were highlighted. Then, on May 26 and 27, the *Train of Tomorrow* made its first non-test run, a 560-mile round trip from Chicago to French Lick, Indiana, on the Monon, with some one hundred travel and industrial writers aboard.

The following day General Motors laid on a luncheon at Chicago's Palmer House for more than a thousand of the city's civic and industrial elite. Festivities then moved to Soldiers' Field where the train, open for inspection, was formally dedicated "as a research project aimed to augment the service of the railroads to the public." Public display lasted most of the next week.

From there the consist went on a nationwide exhibition tour totaling 65,000 miles, including transit of California's Feather River Canyon (too late, as the 30 domes for the future *California Zephyr* had been ordered from Budd earlier in the year). In addition, the train was displayed in both 1948 and 1949 at the Chicago Railroad Fair.

Union Pacific bought the *Train of Tomorrow* in April 1950. Its barnstorming days nearly over, the consist was repainted at Union Pacific's Omaha shops in the road's yellow, gray, and red "Streamliner" scheme but retained the ethereal names provided by GM. E7 No. 765 became UP No. 988. Then the cars sallied forth on UP's own tour, on exhibition under a mammoth banner reading "Train of Tomorrow — Your Portland–Tacoma–Seattle Train of Today." On June 18 they entered Seattle–Portland service, running (in a train amplified by an additional parlor and one or more coaches, all rebuilt heavyweights initially) as UP's contribution to a pool operation of many years' standing between those cities that also involved Great Northern and Northern Pacific. The northbound train for a time also carried sleepers from Chicago and San Francisco.

No doubt UP found the *Train of Tomorrow's* utility limited by its singularity — there was only one of it. A transcontinental schedule may require as many as six sets of equipment, and a pair of consists is required to protect virtually any schedule of consequence, which is to say any schedule worthy of such fine new equipment as the *Train of Tomorrow*. The Portland–Seattle pool train — unnamed, but listed in the timetable as a "Domeliner" during the time it was one — was probably the only place on the UP that a single set of equipment, however grand, made much practical sense.

Train 457 left Portland in the morning and arrived in Seattle around noon; the consist returned to Portland in the afternoon as 458. Throughout its long stint in this pool-train service, sleeper Dream Cloud (which, with observation-lounge Moon Glow, ran into the 1960s) served as a railroad-operated parlor car. A seat in Dream Cloud or in the additional parlor (or a room in the through sleeper) carried admission privileges to Moon Glow. While flat-top coaches were unreserved, coach Star Dust was a reserved-seat car and cost extra.

Changes occurred in the Seattle–Portland service through the years. Lightweights replaced rebuilt heavyweights in 1951. Diner Sky View was the first dome to leave the train, in the fall of 1957, and chair

The *Train of Tomorrow* went touring in the summer and fall of 1947, drawing good crowds wherever it was displayed. (Above, R. L. Kirpatrick: *Trains* Magazine Collection; below, Fred Matthews)

After Union Pacific purchased the *Train of Tomorrow*, the consist looked sharp in the railroad's classic Armour yellow and harbor mist gray. In "pool-train" service for the UP between Portland and Seattle, the four-dome consist was amplified by a through sleeper and parlor car cut in among the domes, and flat-top coaches forward. This is train No. 457, Seattle-bound along Puget Sound. The Tacoma Narrows Bridge is in the background. (Union Pacific Museum Collection)

car Star Dust was removed the following spring. Moon Glow eventually had its solarium end squared off for midtrain operation. Along with its three mates, it was withdrawn from service entirely in the 1960s and hauled to the scrapyard — a fate that even by the mid-1990s had befallen surprisingly few of the *Train of Tomorrow's* 230 descendants. (And Moon Glow, miraculously, was itself spared the torch and is under restoration by the Union Station Museum in Ogden, Utah.)

So *Train of Tomorrow's* Astra Domes had an active life that was short but sweet — sweet at least for the countless thousands of visitors who clambered through the touring *Train of Tomorrow*, filled with post-war optimism about the future of the American streamliner, and sweet for the myriad passengers who rode under glass in these cars during their decade and more in revenue service.

Singleton cars, and no doubt hampered by that inherent liability, Star Dust, Sky View, Dream Cloud, and Moon Glow vanished from the scene roughly three decades ago. But dome cars built more or less in their image, suggested and inspired by these pioneers, are very much alive today.

"MONUMENT TO AN IDEA" HAS A SAFE HOME

In the 1980s, the concept of the dome car declined in currency in the United States as Amtrak retired most of its fleet and opted to make double-deck Superliners the standard in the West. Simultaneously the monument to that idea — a two-legged stone pedestal topped by a scale model of a Vista-Dome that stood in Colorado's Glenwood Canyon — had languished in

In Seattle, the Milwaukee Road's Chicago-bound *Olympian Hiawatha* passes UP's ex-*Train of Tomorrow*. It's July 1951, and domes for the *Olympian Hi* are a little over a year away. (Fred Matthews)

neglect. In 1985 the partially vandalized model was removed for safekeeping by Denver & Rio Grande Western, the builder of the monument. When the 29-ton, 8-foot-tall pedestal was slated for demolition as an improved Interstate 70 was rammed through the canyon, volunteers from various groups, agencies, and companies rallied to save the monument.

A plaque on the monument thoroughly explains its history: "The idea for the Vista-Dome railroad car was conceived on the Denver & Rio Grande Western Railroad across the Colorado River from this point on July 4, 1944. Riding through Glenwood Canyon in the fireman's seat high in the nose of a Rio Grande diesel locomotive built by his company, C. R. Osborn, vice-president of General Motors and general manager of Electro-Motive Division, was struck by the need for giving passengers an unobstructed view of the inspiring scenery overhead and on all sides. The idea of building glass-enclosed domes into the cars occurred to him. Unlike so many originators of unusual new

ideas, Mr. Osborn in a brief five years saw his dream grow into full practical utilization. Vista-Dome *California Zephyr* trains went into service March 21, 1949, between San Francisco and Chicago and now daily pass the spot where the idea was born."

The monument was said to be located at the exact site of Osborn's brainstorm — Grizzly, Colorado, which happened to be the place on the Rio Grande where the *CZs* — No. 17 and No. 18 — met if both were on time. This altar to the Vista-Dome was dedicated on September 15, 1950, with Osborn in attendance, along with D&RGW president Wilson McCarthy.

The monument now stands at the Colorado Railroad Museum in Golden, brought there through the efforts of the museum, the Intermountain Chapter-National Railway Historical Society, and the Rocky Mountain Railroad Club. Flatiron Structures of Longmont, Colorado — builders of the reconstructed Devil's Gate High Bridge, part of the Georgetown Loop, over which tourist trains now run — donated time and

The "Monument to an Idea" — the idea was Cyrus Osborn's brainstorm about dome cars — stood for years in Glenwood Canyon, Colorado. Here the westbound *California Zephyr* with five full-size Vista-Domes rolls by behind a shiny trio of Alco PAs. (Otto Roach: Rio Grande Collection, State Historical Society of Colorado)

equipment to load the stone base on a flatbed truck for transport to the museum. Once it was securely in place, the nine-foot-long, roughly 500-pound Vista-Dome model was lifted back in place by crane, once again a fitting monument to a splendid idea.

ANTEDILUVIAN DOMES

Proving that there's nothing new under the sun, historians could dispute the claim that Osborn's Glenwood Canyon traverse gave rise to the idea of the dome car. In fact, Canadian Pacific Railway, a major player in the modern dome-car era, just after the turn of the century had operated four wooden cars that could be considered primitive domes. All were built by CPR in Montreal; the first came from Hochelaga Shops in 1902, the other three from Angus in 1906.

These curious beasts had a large cupola at each end, and between them a clerestoried center section with broad windows and revolving leather chairs for 14. In the end sections were platforms four feet above the floor level; on each of these were perched four cane-bottomed chairs. Sitting there, passengers could look out in all directions from a cupola projecting three feet above the roof line.

These handsome cars with natural mahogany exteriors were used between Donald and Revelstoke, British Columbia, over the Selkirk Range. They were scrapped in 1913, presumably because the dome car's season had not yet arrived. (In an era before efficient air conditioning and polarizing glass, the sun streaming in through all those windows was apparently too bright and too hot.) Similarly, the railroads had been very slow to embrace the dining car after its introduction in

22

Well ahead of their time were Canadian Pacific's four turn-of-the-century dome cars — called "observation cars," as modern dome cars often are by the uninitiated. Number 86 is seen here. Note that the side cupola windows opened in an attempt to combat the heat. (Canadian Pacific Railroad: *Trains* Magazine Collection)

CPR's early domelike cars appear on a British Columbia Electric Railway special bound for the horse races at Minoru Park in Richmond, just south of downtown Vancouver on BCE's line to Steveston. BCE frequently borrowed CPR equipment for these trains. The distinctive Dick Kerr locomotive up front was built in 1909. (Vancouver Public Library: William D. Middleton Collection)

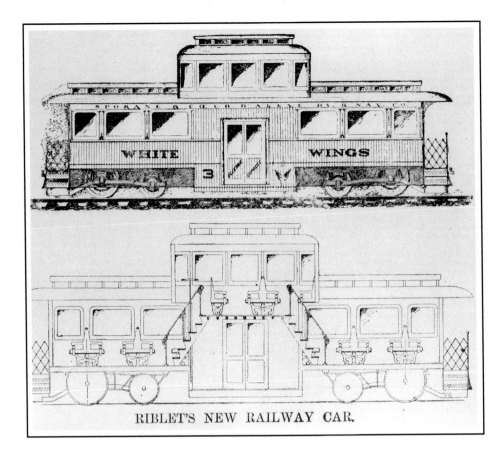

RIBLET'S NEW RAILWAY CAR.

Spokane and Coeur d'Alene Railway and Navigation Company's projected interurban dome car
as it appeared in the *Scientific American Supplement.* (William D. Middleton Collection)

1868. And it's an interesting coincidence that the first diner, Delmonico, was built in Chicago, Burlington & Quincy's Aurora Shops, birthplace of Silver Dome, the first modern dome car.

Forty years after these quasi-domes had been scrapped — and right after Canadian Pacific had ordered 36 new-style domes from Budd for the Canadian and Dominion — the railroad dredged up the old cars from memory and files and claimed to have been the first on the block to own domes. Burlington and others were unimpressed — maintaining that a cupola is not a dome.

Actually, an even more domelike car had been suggested over a decade before CPR's first one was built. This triple dome, sketched in an 1881 issue of *Scientific American,* was the idea of another Canadian — a car-builder from Winnipeg. The rooftop protrusions on this vehicle actually had more in common with the modern dome cars than CPR's cupolas, including glass fronts and tapered, multipaned sides.

A dozen years later, another domelike idea was on the drawing board: "Riblet's New Railway Car," reported and pictured once again by *Scientific American* — in the March 25, 1893, issue, of the *Supplement* in this

case. This car was particularly anomalous in being intended for service under wire on the Spokane & Coeur d'Alene Railway and Navigation company — a 32-mile-long interurban line incorporated in Washington State but never built. (Had it been, it would have been among the country's earliest interurbans.) Designed by B. C. Riblet, the line's chief engineer, the car would have been 40 feet long, with main-level seating, an observation room, and storage for freight and express underneath this observation area.

Powered by two 45-horsepower single-reduction motors, the car was expected to make 40 miles per hour on the level. The motorman would have operated the car from the observation room except when running in the city; then he'd be stationed at controls on the open platform. Called "White Wings" and painted ivory white with gold trim and lettering, this would have been quite the glamorous vehicle. No mention is made of the projected mode of power collection, but either trolley pole or pantograph would seem inconsistent with the tall, clerestory-roofed observation cupola.

So in fact, the modern dome car may have had more than one father — or, if that's impossible, multiple stepfathers or godfathers.

These brochures highlight different dome nomenclature: UP's "Astra Dome" and MP's creative "Planetarium Dome." (Author's Collection, above; Collection of Bob Schmidt, left)

WHAT'S IN A (DOME) NAME?

"A rose by any other name would smell as sweet," said Shakespeare. Yet the railroads, trying to differentiate their own dome cars from those of the competition, relied on creative nomenclature to help in this effort.

The first coinage was "Vista-Dome," the name Chicago, Burlington & Quincy hung on its Silver Dome and the dozens of Budd-built stainless-steel domes to follow. Primogeniture and numerical superiority — CB&Q owned 44 of the 235 domes built in North America — make Vista-Dome the Kleenex of dome-naming, the closest thing to a generic term. Northern Pacific used the moniker, too, for its *North Coast Limited* domes — not surprisingly, since CB&Q was part owner of that fleet. Naturally, Burlington's *California Zephyr* partners Western Pacific and Denver & Rio Grande

Western used the term "Vista-Dome" for their *CZ* cars, and D&RGW also applied it to domes it bought from Chesapeake & Ohio for *Royal Gorge* and later *Yampa Valley Mail* service.

The other early entry — probably, in fact, the earliest in conception if not in execution — was "Astra Dome," the name applied by General Motors to its *Train of Tomorrow* cars. When Union Pacific bought the cars it also adopted the name, which it would use for the 40 domes eventually purchased from American Car & Foundry and Pullman-Standard. UP's trains equipped with these cars officially became "Dome-liners," a play on the term "Streamliner," over which UP claimed some proprietorship.

But it didn't stop there. Among the most creative namers were Missouri Pacific, which dubbed its *Eagle* cars "Planetarium Domes." Baltimore & Ohio called its cars "Strata Domes." On the Santa Fe they were "Pleasure Domes" or "Big Domes," on the Canadian Pacific "Scenic Domes," on the Great Northern "Great Domes," and on the Chicago, Milwaukee, St. Paul & Pacific "Super Domes." When six of these Milwaukee domes went to Canadian National in 1964, they became "Sceneramic" cars.

2

Proliferation
Along the Way of the *Zephyrs*

In December 1947, hard on the heels of the *Train of Tomorrow*, two seven-car consists arrived from the Budd Company (successor to the Edward G. Budd Manufacturing Company, as of the previous year) to become Burlington's twice-daily Chicago–St. Paul–Minneapolis *Twin Zephyrs*. Ten of the 14 cars delivered by Budd for these trains were "Vista-Domes," as Burlington would always call its dome cars. Only the diners and the baggage-club lounge combination cars would be flat-tops.

There were eight dome chair cars — Silver Bluff, Silver Glade, Silver Island, Silver River, Silver Stream, Silver Wave, Silver Scene, and Silver Vision — and a pair of dome parlor-observations, Silver View and Silver Vista. These were the first of the standard Budd "short domes" (versus full-length domes, which would appear later) that over the next decade would achieve a substantial numerical superiority and a well-deserved reputation for excellence.

The cars were much-improved versions of pioneering Silver Dome. Perhaps most significantly, they were the first domes with curved glass. Like Silver Dome, the cars carried 24 seats above. But the new coaches accommodated 54 below, much more profitable than Silver Dome's 34, and all arranged in normal forward-facing coach style, while the area under the dome was depressed and used for washrooms. The pair of tail cars had dome areas identical to the chair cars, parlor seats on the main floor, and drawing room below. "Nature smiles 300 miles" on the *Twin Zephyr* route, according to company publicity, and the domes proved the perfect vantage for passengers to take it all in.

Designing these domes was no simple matter. Budd faced substantial hurdles, as did Pullman-

Standard in designing the *Train of Tomorrow* cars and those that followed. Clearance restrictions were an ever-present problem, requiring that the dome extend no more than 28 inches above the normal roof line and that the floor drop no more than 18 inches below normal. This lowered floor required specially designed water tanks, air-brake reservoirs, and air-conditioning equipment to fit the tighter underbody space. At the same time, the expansive glass of the dome increased the car's air-conditioning need by 24 percent over a standard coach.

The biggest problem was basic structural integrity. In Budd's patented Shotwelded construction, the roof and full sides — not just the floor and walls up to the windows, as was more typically the case — were integrally important in carrying the load of the car and withstanding compressive forces. With the continuity of the roof line broken by the dome, a major redistribution of stress was required, accomplished by very substantial structural partitions at the ends of the dome to distribute the stress broadly, extra-strong glass in the dome, and reinforced longitudinal members at the juncture of roof and side.

On March 11, 1947, to see that all these engineering challenges had been adequately met, the first Vista-Dome car from the Burlington order — completed except for the trim — was tested by the Budd Company at its Philadelphia plant, with a large number of railroad executives in attendance. At the firm's railway test laboratory, the car was subjected to stresses of four kinds: an 800,000-pound compression load at coupler height, a 500,000-pound compression load at buffer height, jacking at diagonally opposite bolster pads, and jacking at diagonally opposite corners.

The 1947 *Twin Zephyrs* were remarkably long on domes as originally configured. In this early view crossing Great Northern's lovely Stone Arch Bridge at Minneapolis-St. Paul, a veteran shovel-nose *Zephyr* unit is pinch-hitting for the train's usual slant-nose E5A. (George Miles Ryan Studio)

All went well. Soon sister cars began to roll off the line and, by year's end, into service on the *Twin Zephyrs*. These luxurious cars had carpeted floors, molded luggage racks, and both venetian blinds and curtains at the windows. The dome-bulkhead wall in the forward seating section presented a large unbroken expanse and thus became the favored mural area on Budd domes. The *Twin Zephyr* coaches featured murals such as "Father Marquette and Joliet on the Mississippi, 1673." The bulkhead in the parlor-observation carried an illustrated map of the train's route.

Just months after the 1947 *Twin Zephyr's* inaugural, domes began to arrive from Budd that would eventually make up the Burlington-Rio Grande-Western Pacific *California Zephyr;* they'd been ordered back in October 1945, one month later than the *Twin Zephyr's* cars. This Chicago–Denver–Salt Lake City–Oakland service, which many would come to consider the ultimate dome train, would be inaugurated on March 20, 1949. Meanwhile, as Vista-Dome chair cars arrived from the builder, some as much as a year in advance, they were placed in service on the *Exposition Flyer,* the

heavyweight train the *CZ* would replace. By the summer of 1948, dome coaches were a consistent, advertised feature of the *Flyer.*

Six *CZ* consists were necessary to protect the train's leisurely wanderings through California's Feather River Canyon and Colorado's Rockies. Each was 11 cars long and included three Vista-Dome coaches, a Vista-Dome dormitory-buffet lounge (which originally was generically Western but in 1957 would be restyled to incorporate the famous Cable Car Room), and a Vista-Dome sleeper-buffet lounge-observation. This totaled 30 domes, of which 13 were owned by CB&Q, 11 by WP, and six by D&RGW — numbers based on shares of the total route mileage. In 1952 would come a thirty-first dome, the seventh Vista-Dome obs, which when pooled with the rest of the *CZ* obs fleet, utilizing that train's Chicago layover time, protected both legs of the overnight Chicago–Lincoln, Nebraska, *Ak-Sar-Ben Zephyr.* (This train's curious handle, Nebraska spelled backward, dates from the heavyweight era.) All the *CZ* cars had Silver-prefix names, by then a well-established *Zephyr* tradition

Silver Feather's official portrait. All *California Zephyr* cars carried the train's name on the letter-boards, with the owning railroad's initials in smaller letters at the car ends. *CZ* cars continued the *Zephyr* tradition of Silver-prefix names — and of applying names to coaches, diners, lounges, even baggage cars, as well as sleepers. (W. H. Hoedt Studios: Peter Tilp Collection)

derived from the trains' invariable dress of unadorned stainless steel.

The *Twin Zephyr's* dome proliferation — five of seven cars in the consist — was an embarrassment of riches for a daytime train, never equaled. Likewise, the *California Zephyr* with five domes in its consist was the all-time leader among the long-hauls (in cars if not in number of dome seats, where the *Empire Builder* would lead). The observation car's dome was reserved for Pullman passengers, as was the midtrain buffet lounge's, though the lounge itself was largely patronized by coach travelers, who had the three chair-car domes for their use.

Still more *Zephyr* domes were to come from Budd, but not until after a hiatus of nearly four years. On February 1, 1953, the *Kansas City Zephyr*, a new train, entered daytime service between Kansas City and Chicago. The catalyst was the more direct route that the newly opened Brookfield–Kansas City Shortline afforded. "Shorter, smoother, faster," blurbed the brochure introducing the *Kansas City Zephyr* and overnight running mate, also new, the *American Royal Zephyr*. "The new Kansas City Short-Cut levels the hills, straightens the curves and cuts the mileage, making possible finer and faster passenger service between Chicago and Kansas City." Also called the "Centennial Cut-off," this upgraded route was a $16-million project that involved rehabilitation of 22 miles of existing Carrollton Branch trackage and all-new construction totaling 48.4 miles.

In each of the *Kansas City Zephyr's* two six-car consists were a Vista-Dome chair-dormitory-buffet lounge and a Vista-Dome parlor-observation. The chair-dormitory-buffet lounges were also used on the *American Royal Zephyr*, keeping them rolling virtually 24 hours a day.

Inaugural festivities for the new trains filled the last week in January and ranged across the route, from endpoint to endpoint. In Chicago on a Saturday, Burlington ran five 90-minute round-trip excursions to Aurora; tickets were $1 apiece. On January 21 the "Queen of American Royal," Judith Anderson of Liberty, Missouri, christened the trains by breaking champagne over the *Kansas City Zephyr's* dome-observation and the *American Royal Zephyr's* E-unit diesel — it had no obs car.

Then, in October 1956, a new *Denver Zephyr* became the last major streamliner re-equipping in pre-Amtrak America. Each of the train's consists featured a Vista-Dome coach, a Vista-Dome dormitory-buffet lounge (the noted Chuck Wagon car, with Western theme), and a Vista-Dome parlor-buffet lounge-observation.

The vast fleet of *Zephyr* domes — 53 in total, when all *CZ* cars are tallied, including WP's and D&RGW's — were much of a piece, both inside and out, but subtle variations reflected differing requirements of different services. The one constant was the dome area, which always contained 24 seats arranged in forward-facing rows of four across. Style and finish were also constants.

On February 1, 1953, the first *Kansas City Zephyr* heads west out of Kansas City Union Station before going around the gooseneck and and pointing toward Chicago. (Ronald Christinson: *Trains* Magazine Collection)

Though the daytime *Twin Zephyr's* 54 chair-car seats were reduced to 46 on the more spacious long-haul *CZ* (and 50 on the overnight *DZ*), the pure coaches among the domes were all clearly cousins. In all cases the area under the domes was devoted to rest rooms. But there were differences in interior decor. On the dome bulkhead of each of the 18 *CZ* cars' forward coach section, for instance, was an original mural by Connecticut artist Mary Lawser. These murals were on regional themes: the Rio Grande's narrow gauge through the mountains, the Mormon emigration of 1847, gold panning in California, the "Pike's Peak or bust" trek. These oil-on-canvas murals became a staple of Budd short domes built for the *Zephyrs* and were a way of individualizing a basically homogeneous product.

With their sleek, graceful bullet ends, the seven *CZ* observations — Silver Horizon, Silver Penthouse, Silver Solarium, Silver Lookout, Silver Sky, Silver Crescent, and Silver Planet — looked at first glance from the outside much like the *Twin Zephyrs'* Silver View and Silver Vista. But the *CZ* cars carried their domes aft of center and the *Twin Zephyrs* forward.

The *CZ's* observations — which would be virtually duplicated some five years later in Canadian Pacific's 18 observation cars for *Canadian* and *Dominion* service — were exquisite. They were, as a Budd Company promotional booklet proclaimed, "The car that had everything." For starters, they carried, in addition to three double bedrooms, the train's only drawing room. This luxurious accommodation offered two lowers and one upper berth — and a private shower, placing it in very elite company.

The lounge in the boat-tail was ringed with club chairs facing inward for conversation — plus, at the far end, a pair of rearward-facing settees with fine retrospective views. The snug under-dome cocktail bar had a Russell Patterson mural wrapped around bulkhead and side wall and a stylish hand-carved linoleum bar front.

Denver Zephyr tail cars Silver Chateau and Silver Veranda, on the other hand, were externally akin to *Kansas City Zephyr's* Silver Terrace and Silver Tower (which in later years also showed up on the *Twin Zephyrs*); all four were blunt-end. Like the *Twin Zephyrs'* round-end cars, all offered a drawing room and parlor

29

Budd basically used a cookie cutter in turning out domes for the various *Zephyrs* — and for other trains, for that matter. Hand-painted bulkhead murals were one way of personalizing cars that otherwise were much the same. Here, Philadelphia artist Kathryn Fligg and Budd architect William Chandler flank her mural on a parlor-dome-observation for the *Twin Zephyr*. The painting commemorates Burlington's introduction of the first railway post office car in 1862. (Lawrence S. Williams: *Trains* Magazine Collection)

seats — 31 for the *TZ,* 27 for the *KCZ,* and 11 for the *DZ,* the latter allowing for lounge space at the rear of the car for sleeping-car and parlor-car passengers. The *Kansas City Zephyr's* and *Twin Zephyrs'* tail cars had nothing but swiveling parlor chairs on the main level, with rest rooms and a day drawing room below the dome. Tucked under the *Denver Zephyr's* dome was something grander: the Colorado Room, a handsomely appointed cocktail bar.

Kansas City Zephyr/American Royal Zephyr's Vista-Dome chair-dormitory-buffet lounges Silver Garden and Silver Patio and *DZ's* dormitory-buffet lounges Silver Cup and Silver Kettle were variations on the *CZ* theme played out in dormitory buffet-lounges Silver Club, Silver Lounge, Silver Roundup, Silver Shop,

Silver Chalet, and Silver Hostel. The *DZ* cars were particularly notable as "Chuck Wagon" diners for light meals, with a 19-seat coffee shop plus counter seating for eight and, behind that counter, a galley adequate to serve fairly elaborate hot meals: pan-fried steak, filet of fish, fried chicken.

Silver Garden and Silver Patio packed many functions between buffers. At the forward end was a 24-seat coach section, with a tiny three-tier crew dormitory and toilet tucked in. Under the dome was a six-passenger lounge and the service buffet. Aft was a 17-seat coffee shop.

The coffee-shop section of the "Chuck Wagons" was similar to that aboard the *Kansas City Zephyr/American Royal Zephyr* cars, but a bulkhead

Far more elaborate than Silver Garden and Silver Patio were Silver Kettle and Silver Cup, the *DZ's* "Chuck Wagon" cars, which came along three years later. The cowboy theme was expressed in the mural, "DZ" brands on the tabletops and carvings, as well as the menus and china. (Hedrich-Blessing, Burlington Route: *Trains* Magazine Collection)

mural of a chuck-wagon scene and wall-mounted carvings depicting cowboy life gave the *Denver Zephyr* cars a decidedly Western personality. A "DZ" branding iron adorned the Formica-topped tables. Playful, cutout menus had appropriately Western graphics and told the story of the real chuck wagons that served cowboys on roundup. Special china carried the "DZ" brand.

These cars were so well received on their introduction in 1956 that, the following year, the *CZ* partners decided to remodel the food- and beverage-service areas of that train's somewhat nondescript Vista-Dome dormitory buffet-lounge into the Cable Car Room. Goals were twofold: to provide the kind of distinctive regional personality that had proved a hit in

the Chuck Wagons, and to upgrade the buffet to allow a more extensive menu to be served.

With photomurals and models of those famous San Francisco conveyances, and the room itself redesigned to replicate the interior of one, complete with bellpull, the renovation was a big success, and the Cable Car Room became one of the *CZ's* hallmarks in its later years. Though a galley as elaborate as the Chuck Wagon's was deemed prohibitively expensive, addition of a hot plate and steam table allowed what had been primarily a beverage-service car to move into the light-meal business. This took some pressure off the diner, a main objective of the renovation.

Like the *Zephyr* fleet in general, its Vista-Dome component was remarkable for scope, quality, and

In September 1961, the eastbound *Morning Zephyr* leaves Rochelle, Illinois, with its dome complement somewhat depleted and two heavyweight coaches in the consist but carrying its original dome-observation. (Howard Patrick)

consistency. From the *Pioneer Zephyr's* creation in 1934 right through the final *Denver Zephyr* of 1956, this was an amazing collection of trains and cars. Exclusively Budd-built (astounding in itself, reflecting a loyalty unique among major passenger-carriers), this armada was all dazzling stainless steel, ornamented only with black lettering in an Art Deco style that was a perfection of understated elegance. Among this vast array of chair cars, sleepers, lounges, parlors, diners, and observations, the 53 Vista-Domes were the crown jewels. Following are sketches of the most illustrious trains to carry them.

TWIN ZEPHYRS: THE TRUE PIONEERS

Throughout the lightweight era, the *Twin Zephyrs* have been in the forefront. The trains were born on April 17, 1935, as three-car, articulated "pocket streamliners" running between Chicago and the Twin Cities. They were essentially identical to the original *Zephyr* of 1934, soon to be called the *Pioneer Zephyr* to distinguish it from a growing fleet of sisters. It was these first trains that established the famous Budd-Burlington

hallmarks that would later be replicated so often and so successfully: Shotwelded, fluted-stainless-steel cars with smart black lettering.

Demand for seats continued to grow, so the very next year the tiny *Twin Zephyrs* — already augmented by the addition of another coach — were replaced by a much more substantial pair of integrated trainsets, these seven cars long (including the power unit). While the original "pocket" *Twin Zephyrs* had only eight-seat dinettes and small parlor sections in the round end of the observation cars, the new consists were far more luxurious, featuring two parlor cars and a 40-seat diner (plus a 16-seat dinette, when another coach was added in 1937).

These trains carried on for 11 years in the highly competitive Chicago–Twin Cities market — going head-to-head with Milwaukee Road's *Hiawathas* and Chicago & North Western's *400s*. Then, once more in the vanguard, the *Twin Zephyrs* were reborn yet again — this time as the first domeliner in regular service. The domes were put to good use on the *Twin Zephyrs,* since for most of the run — the 282 miles between Savanna, Illinois, and St. Paul — the trains followed

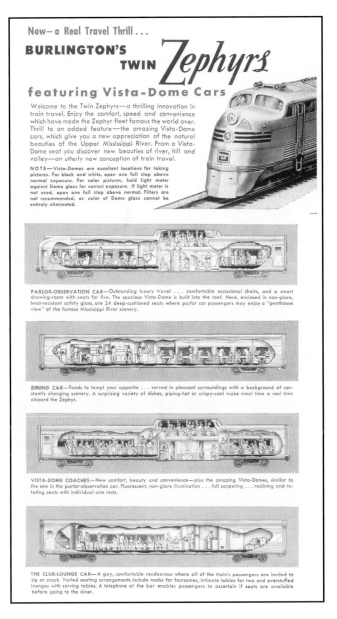

"Where nature smiles 300 miles" was the *Twin Zephyrs'* venue, according to this brochure. (Peter Tilp Collection)

the Mississippi River. "It is somehow fitting," read the train's brochure, "that 'Old Man River' should be the first to greet the most modern of trains — the *Twin Zephyrs* which feature the thrilling Vista-Dome cars." And they did what they were expected to do for the bottom line. In 1940, the *Twins* had returned a very respectable 59 percent of gross as income. For 1948, the first full year of dome operation, that number leapt to a remarkable 72.4 percent.

Between Chicago and St. Paul, as it happened, Great Northern's *Empire Builder*, Northern Pacific's *North Coast Limited*, and the eastbound *Morning Zephyr* and westbound *Afternoon Zephyr* ran on roughly similar schedules. This opened the possibility of various consist

combinations for the run along the Mississippi, which Burlington seized during the mid-sixties, when patronage began dramatic declines. Combinations were initially of just two trains, and only out of season, with the cars sorting out into three distinct consists and schedules for the peak summer months. For the winter of 1967–68, however, all three trains became one, and (except for weekends) stayed that way year-round. This meant a train with an extraordinary array of dome cars.

The *Twin Zephyrs* soldiered on right up to Amtrak, when their Chicago–Twin Cities route lost out in the selection process to the Milwaukee Road's. But for a last hurrah — in the summer of 1970, the final one before Amtrak — the combined *Twin Zephyr-North Coast Limited-Empire Builder* consist racked up what must be the all-time record for dome-car proliferation. The *Zephyr* piece included two dome coaches, the Builder piece three dome coaches and a full-length dome lounge, and the North Coast Limited piece two dome coaches and two dome sleepers. One train, 20 cars altogether, ten domes.

CALIFORNIA ZEPHYR: "THE MOST TALKED ABOUT TRAIN IN AMERICA"

Of all the streamliners, the *California Zephyr* could be the one most closely associated with dome cars. To start with, it had so many of them — and so much to see through their windows, kept clean by two en-route washings. For another, it was born a domeliner, rather than made one by the addition of dome cars to a service already in operation. In this respect it stood almost alone, joined only by far more modest fleetmates *Kansas City Zephyr* and *American Royal Zephyr* and Canadian Pacific's *Canadian*, a train remarkably like the *CZ*. On all other dome trains the domes were, if you will, an afterthought.

And what souvenir better characterizes the whole dome-car enterprise than "Vista-Dome Views," the mileage-keyed pamphlet of along-the-way details distributed aboard the train throughout its 21-year career. "Beauty by day . . . all the way," read the earliest version of this brochure. "The *California Zephyr* is the only transcontinental train between the Great Lakes and the Golden Gate which has been scheduled to give travelers the choicest of western scenery by day." Indeed, the Colorado Rockies and California's Feather River Canyon were hard to beat. As time wore on and the economics of its operation deteriorated, this document evolved from two-color staplebound booklet to a large single-sheet folder in brown ink, but it survived to the bitter end.

On November 22, 1964, a spare *CZ* observation was pressed into service on a Chicago–Rockford excursion behind Burlington Mikado No. 4960. The train was not wyed at Rockford, putting the obs right behind the locomotive's canteen for the return trip. (Jim Boyd)

And the end was bitter. Western Pacific (eventually joined by partner Rio Grande) first asked the Interstate Commerce Commission for permission to discontinue the *CZ* in September 1966; though some 40 months later the ICC finally said yes, the intervening proceedings had been so passionate, provocative, rancorous, and prominent that both politicians and the public were alerted to the crisis in passenger railroading. It's often and easily argued that the loss of the *CZ* led directly to the creation of Amtrak.

All this heartache and intrigue of the train's final days was far away when, on a sunny afternoon in March 1949 on San Francisco's Embarcadero, actress Eleanor Parker (whose fame has perhaps not held up as well as the *CZ's*) broke a bottle of California Champagne over the feather-bedecked nose of Western Pacific F3 No. 802.

"I christen thee the *California Zephyr*," she said, taking the final step in the protracted birth of a train that would survive remarkably unchanged over the exactly 21 years of its pre-Amtrak operation. Year after year the three Vista-Dome chair cars and Vista-Dome buffet-lounge (always marshaled together, a dizzying array of domes just in front of the diner) and the splendid Vista-Dome lounge-observation (at the train's end, with a fetching tailsign that featured an illuminated etching of the Golden Gate Bridge on yellow-orange glass) were part of the consist, as inevitable as death and taxes but far nicer. The train proved an unparalleled success, with the average occupancy in its first decade of service an extraordinary 89.4 percent over the central portion of the route.

Every day, once in each direction, this plethora of domes paraded through Glenwood Canyon, where

The Zephyrette and photography from the dome, two *CZ* hallmarks, are depicted on the cover of this 1955 brochure. (Author's Collection)

GM's Cyrus Osborn had gotten the dome-car bug. The Vista-Dome was literally put on a pedestal there — a model, as a "monument to an idea." Naturally, "Vista-Dome Views" called it to travelers' attention, as did an announcement read over the public address system by the Zephyrette — or stewardess, an important personage aboard the *California Zephyr* throughout its history.

Though maintenance and service standards naturally slipped in the *CZ's* final, travail-filled season, the train remained a noble venture right up to the end, when protesters came to trackside to mourn the streamliners' demise with signs reading "Western Pathetic" and "Hey, Dad — What's a passenger train?" The ICC called the *California Zephyr* "a unique national asset," and few who gawked at Glenwood Canyon or Feather River Canyon from its domes, dined on Rocky Mountain brook trout in its stylish diner, or snacked in the Cable Car Room would disagree.

A significant ghost of the illustrious *CZ* lingered for a dozen years longer, thanks to D&RGW's decision not

The *CZ's* domes were washed twice en route: At Denver (shown here) and at Portola, California. (W. A. Akin: *Trains* Magazine Collection)

to join Amtrak at the passenger corporation's start-up in 1971. This triggered the triweekly Denver–Salt Lake City *Rio Grande Zephyr,* a much-loved little train that would write the final important chapter in the book of dome operations by private railroads in the United States. On this *California Zephyr* remnant, Rio Grande fielded all its former *CZ* equipment except the sleepers, which meant five Vista-Domes in peak season. This kept the flame alive until 1983, when Denver & Rio Grande Western finally threw in the towel and let

its pocket domeliner disappear in the wake of an Amtrak-operated Superliner *CZ.*

DENVER ZEPHYR: THE LAST GREAT NEWBUILDING

When the *Denver Zephyr* first hit the rails on November 8, 1936, it represented another step in the *Zephyr* evolution: an overnight train, with sleepers. Otherwise the 12-car consists were much akin to the second *Twin*

This brochure from 1963 promotes Colorado Springs as the *DZ's* ultimate destination. (William F. Howes, Jr., Collection)

Zephyrs, delivered from Budd just after the *DZ*. A classic "shovel-nose" diesel, so much a part of the original *Zephyr* look, was once again on the point. The new *DZ* consist was only partially articulated, however, allowing separation at numerous points, the first *Zephyr* to offer this flexibility.

And it was the *DZ* that began a *Zephyr* tradition that carried right through the dome era: the prefix "Silver" in all car names. The *Pioneer Zephyr* and the first *Twins* had carried numbers only, while the second *Twins* were named for Greek gods and goddesses. But from the 1936 *DZ* onward, Burlington's silver trains would always be made up of "Silver" cars.

Another innovation on the original *DZ* were "Zephyrettes" — the stewardess-nurses who would become most famous later on the *California Zephyr*.

This first *DZ* offered streamlined luxury at its best, with diner, cocktail lounge, dinette, coaches, sleeping accommodations that included sections, roomettes, chambrettes, double bedrooms, compartments, and drawing rooms, and parlor seats in the round-end buffet observation car. These consists had remarkable longevity in *DZ* service, just a few days short of 20 years. Then on October 28, 1956, the new domed *DZ* arrived, allowing the old trains to head off in a different direction from Denver Union Station, taking over as the *Texas Zephyr* to Dallas.

The 1956 *Denver Zephyr* was notable in a number of ways, including the introduction of Slumbercoaches, the budget sleeping rooms that were the pre-Amtrak

passenger railroads' last gasp at innovation. And as it turned out, these two 14-car consists — all new except for the baggage and baggage-mail cars — would be the last complete passenger trains built in America by the private railroads.

Domes were a key feature of the *DZ*, though it was basically an overnight service and stopped at Denver, just when the scenery started to get good. The consists included three domes — the blunt-end dome parlor-buffet observation, a dome coach, and the dome dormitory-buffet lounge that gained fame as the "Chuck Wagon."

Another innovation of the 1956 train was that part of the consist — a flat-top coach, the Chuck-Wagon dome, one of the two Slumbercoaches, and a ten-roomette, six-double-bedroom sleeper — ran through Denver to Colorado Springs in the consist of the *Royal Gorge*, which also had a dome, purchased from the Chesapeake & Ohio. (Later the *DZ's* dome-coach ran through in lieu of the Chuck Wagon car.) While it paralleled rather than assaulted the Front Range of the Rockies, this 75-mile run did provide some fine views. So the *DZ* was the last of the new *Zephyrs*, the end of a long silver line that had begun in 1934 with the *Pioneer*. With its Slumbercoaches, it was also the end of the line for passenger-car evolution in the era before Amtrak.

And the *DZ* effectively represented the end of the line for dome-car development, too, embodying the final new directions. In its midtrain Chuck Wagons and its parlor-observations featuring the Colorado Room,

It's March 24, 1974, near Gilluly, Utah, where the eastbound *Rio Grande Zephyr* meets Rio Grande Extra 3091 West. The *RGZ's* unusual lash-up of freight power plus former Alco PB steam car 253 results from an extra-long consist honoring the 25th anniversary of the *California Zephyr* on Rio Grande rails. (Ted Benson)

Silver Chateau carries the markers, and the *Denver Zephyr* tailsign, as the *DZ* rolls west through Highlands, Illinois, in July 1969. The slumbercoach is tucked in right behind the dome obs. (Peter Tilp)

Typically Budd would herald its new streamliners with a series of ads featuring the art of Leslie Regan, an Iowa-born illustrator who specialized in transportation subjects. Here Silver Terrace brings up the rear of the *Kansas City Zephyr.* (Author's Collection)

the Burlington had created novel dome cars with cosmetically distinctive spaces. The only subsequent domes from any builder would be six dome coaches delivered by Pullman-Standard in 1958 to Union Pacific and Wabash for *City of St. Louis* service — virtual duplicates of earlier American Car & Foundry domes.

The launch of the Vista-Dome *Denver Zephyrs* so late in the passenger-train era was a statement of hope and confidence by a railroad loath to give up on passengers. And for a good while, swimming against the tide, the *DZ* performed up to expectations. Along with the domes, the Slumbercoaches were a hit, showing a remarkable 83.6 percent occupancy rate over the first five years.

The *DZ* remained one of the survivors, rolling right up to Amtrak with consist virtually intact. Though the Chuck Wagon was borrowed for a Chicago–Ogden "California Service" remnant of the discontinued *CZ,* the rest remained: "Colorado Room" Vista-Dome parlor-observation (though run midtrain), Vista-Dome coach, Slumbercoach, sleepers — pretty much the train the planners had in mind back in the early fifties.

3

Budd's Short Domes
The Classic

Though the *Zephyr* fleet was far-flung, not all Budd-built domes for the Burlington wore stainless-steel dress or ran in *Zephyr* consists. Two famous streamliners of the Northwest, Northern Pacific's *North Coast Limited* and Great Northern's *Empire Builder,* claimed CB&Q as their eastern operator, from the Twin Cities to Chicago. Since Burlington participated in the equipment pool for these trains, it's not surprising that the domes carried by both were Budd products.

In 1954 the *North Coast Limited* received ten Vista-Dome chair cars and ten Vista-Dome sleepers with four roomettes, four duplex singles, and four double bedrooms. Ownership of each group of ten was split

Northern Pacific's dome sleepers were a unique design. (Lawrence S. Williams, Inc.: Joseph M. Welsh Collection.)

During many winters, some NP sleeper domes ran in seasonal service on Illinois Central's *City of Miami*. (Roger E. Puta: Melvern Finzer Collection)

the same way: Northern Pacific seven, Burlington two, and Spokane, Portland & Seattle (over which the Pasco, Washington–Portland section of the train ran) one. One dome coach and one dome sleeper operated to Seattle, with one of each going to Portland as well. (In 1957 an eleventh, protection dome coach was purchased by NP, and an additional dome sleeper too.)

The coaches were basically copies of the *California Zephyr's* dome chair cars, with 46 reclining, leg-rest seats on the main level and rest rooms under the domes. The finish was somewhat more spartan, however: linoleum rather than carpeting on floors, curtainless windows with shades rather than venetian blinds, open luggage racks. On the bulkheads were illustrations — less rich in appearance than the oil-on-canvas murals of *Zephyr* cars — of objects indigenous to trains or to NP's territory. (One car, for instance, had sketches of such railroad artifacts as a conductor's cap and punch.) An identifying touch on all the NP Vista-Domes was the speaker grille in the dome, which was formed in the shape of the railroad's

distinctive monad emblem, the Chinese yin and yang.

If the coaches were *Zephyr*-derivative, the sleepers were literally unique cars, unlike any others ever built. And both coaches and sleepers differed significantly from their *Zephyr* brothers in external appearance. Rather than unadorned fluted stainless steel, the cars wore two-tone green paint over flat side panels, the better to blend in with the Pullman-Standard-built cars they were joining in the *North Coast Limited* consist.

Curiously, some of the dome sleepers for a number of years led two lives. In the fall of 1959, the Portland dome sleeper was withdrawn, freeing the cars for other uses — including operation under lease on a pair of Chicago–Florida streamliners, the Illinois Central's *City of Miami* and the Pennsylvania Railroad's *South Wind*. The cars ran on the Pennsy trains in green NP garb, but that year and later — in the mid and late sixties — for their Illinois Central lives they were cloaked in IC's handsome chocolate-and-orange livery.

The two trains operated on alternating, complementary dates, between them providing daily service

41

THIS IS THE TRAIN THAT HAS EVERYTHING!

It is the only train between Chicago and the North Pacific Coast that offers you the attention of a friendly Stewardess-Nurse. Other extras, too . . . 4 Vista-Domes . . . the fascinating new Traveller's Rest buffet-lounge . . . truly superb meals. This train is Northern Pacific's renowned Vista-Dome North Coast Limited.

The view's terrific on Northern Pacific! Send now for "Northwest Adventure", free booklet of scenic trips to or from the Northwest and California. Write G. W. Rodine, 246 Northern Pacific Railway, St. Paul 1, Minnesota.

Luxury has a western flavor in the handsome, colorful "Traveller's Rest" buffet-lounge!

VISTA-DOME
North Coast Limited

One of the world's *EXTRA FINE* trains . . . no extra fare!

NORTHERN PACIFIC RAILWAY

CHICAGO · TWIN CITIES · SPOKANE · PORTLAND · TACOMA · SEATTLE

The *California Zephyr's* Zephyrettes were perhaps better known, but the *North Coast Limited's* stewardess-nurses were much publicized as well. (Author's Collection)

Spokane, Portland & Seattle dome sleeper No. 306 — the only one SP&S owned, as its contribution to the *North Coast Limited* pool — wears recently applied home road colors as it pauses in Missoula, Montana, in June 1970, not long after the Burlington Northern merger and not long before Amtrak. This car would eventually wear Rio Grande livery as Ansco Investments' private car California. (Roger Cook)

from Chicago to Miami. The *City of Miami* ran over IC, Central of Georgia, Atlantic Coast Line, and Florida East Coast rails, and the South Wind over PRR, Louisville & Nashville, ACL, and FEC. (In both cases, the trains moved to Seaboard Air Line from FEC on January 1, 1963, after the latter road was hit with a violent strike.)

Cars were leased for the 1959–60 Florida season, then each winter from 1963–64 through 1967–68 (though in the course of this last year IC put dome coaches newly acquired from Missouri Pacific on the *City of Miami*, while the NP cars remained on the *South Wind*). In summer the domes would be repatriated, with those in IC colors being repainted into NP greens.

For the summer of 1960 the peripatetic domes bounced between different sleeper lines on the *North Coast Limited*: Chicago–Billings and St. Paul–Seattle. (Operation in these rather than a full Chicago–West Coast line may have occurred because No. 307, one of

the trio of sleepers leased that first year, was apparently not returned to NP colors and service until the following May, 1961, leaving inadequate cars to protect a Chicago-to-Pacific line.) When the dome sleepers came home in subsequent summers, they settled down either on the Chicago–Portland sleeper line or as a second dome sleeper on Chicago–Seattle.

One major change that went beyond paint came to the Northern Pacific's fleet of dome sleepers in the spring of 1967, when NP added a "Lounge in the Sky" to six of these cars, providing cocktail seating at tables in the dome for Pullman passengers. This modification, which allowed the train's observation-lounges to be eliminated, required removal of duplex single rooms E and F to free up space under the dome for the service buffet. The work, which cost about $20,000 per car, was done at the Pullman Company's Calumet Shops.

The cars chosen for conversion were Northern Pacific's 307, 308, 311, 312, and 314, and Burlington's

GN dome coach at St. Paul on July 4, 1961 (John S. Ingles)

304. (The 312 and 314 were at that time in winter lease to the Pennsylvania and 304 to the Illinois Central.) Work began at the end of January and ended in May. Initially the plan had been for these Lounge-in-the-Sky cars to run at the end of the consist, like the observation cars they were replacing, but without any external modifications. "It is not intended," as J. A. Cannon, NP's chief mechanical officer, wrote to Pullman in November 1966, "that any changes be provided in the vestibule end for a rounded appearance."

Great Northern — NP's fiercest competitor — was the last of the major passenger railroads in the Northwest to embrace domes. By November 1953, when GN president John M. Budd (son of Burlington's Ralph Budd, a great dome-car booster) announced a 22-dome order for the *Empire Builder* costing about $6 million, the competing Milwaukee Road had already been operating Pullman-Standard-built full-length Super Domes for close to a year on its Chicago–Seattle–Tacoma *Olympian Hiawatha*, and the *North Coast Limited's* domes were on the way.

An interesting sidelight: Ralph Budd had written his directors on August 9, 1945, to report that orders would be placed for the Vista-Dome-heavy *Twin*

Zephyrs. The same letter also mentioned an order for the 12 cars that were CB&Q's share of a new (and, for a number of years to come, domeless) *Empire Builder*. Apparently influential GN directors persisted in the view that domes were an expensive luxury and not necessary in the competition for passengers in the Northwest.

But if GN was slow jumping in, it made quite a splash when it finally leapt. Each of the Empire Builder's five consists would get three short coach domes, and one full-length dome lounge for the exclusive use of Pullman passengers. With four domes regularly assigned, the *Builder* fell one short of the *CZ's* five. But for total seats under glass, GN held the record — 147 to 120 for the *CZ*, since the full-length dome had more than double the capacity of a short dome.

All the *Builder's* domes were Budd products, and the order included one extra of each type beyond those needed to protect the normal consist, which allowed the cars to be rotated out for shopping. Of the 16 short domes, GN owned 12, CB&Q three, and SP&S one; of the six full-length domes, five were GN's and one CB&Q's. GN's domes were similar to NP's in having paneled sides rather than fluted, since they too

44

The combined *North Coast Limited* and *Empire Builder* carry no fewer than seven domes running eastbound at Oregon, Illinois. (Jim Boyd)

would be painted — in GN's fetching Omaha orange and Pullman green streamliner scheme.

Interiors were distinguished by colorful, assertive Indian pictographs on all the bulkheads. Floors were linoleum, but windows featured venetian blinds and curtains with bright Indian designs.

Though trains completely or partially under Burlington's aegis were responsible for a substantial majority of Budd domes sold in the United States — 95 of 122 all told — other roads were customers, too. The earliest was Missouri Pacific, which in June 1948 had received three dome coaches, virtually identical to the *California Zephyr* cars, primarily for the St. Louis–Denver *Colorado Eagle,* a streamliner that had been inaugurated in 1942. These 70-seat "Planetarium Domes" — with 46 "revenue" places on the main floor, the same as for the *CZ* — were part of $14 million in new equipment, 134 cars in all, for the *Eagle* fleet.

These domes were indeed handsome. The roof was unpainted stainless steel, while the letterboard was blue, separated from the roof by a band of cream on the roof rail. The window panel was gray and the side below the windows blue, with gray repeated on the skirt. The belt rail was unpainted stainless, and the cream was repeated on the skid rail, between side and skirt — all in all, a remarkably intricate and attractive

scheme. (Sides were fluted stainless, not paneled, though the livery was virtually fully painted.)

Then in February 1950 Wabash inaugurated a new daytime domeliner that was nearly a dead ringer for the *Twin Zephyrs* (minus one dome coach): the Chicago–St. Louis *Blue Bird,* also built entirely by Budd. The train cost about $1.5 million, including the locomotive: Electro-Motive Division E7 No. 1002, with the name "Blue Bird" bannered across its flanks. Scheduling permitted protection of the service by just a single six-car consist, which included three dome chair cars, each seating 54 on the main floor (20 forward and 34 aft) and the standard 24 in the dome; and a dome parlor-observation with nine seats in a forward parlor section, 14 in a rear parlor section, five in an under-dome drawing room, and six in lounge seats in the round solarium end. This yielded parlor and coach seating for 190, plus 186 nonrevenue seats that included 96 in domes and the six in the observation. A dining car seated 40 at table and offered a 12-seat cocktail lounge. Forward, a baggage-lunch counter-lounge provided another 32 places, all making the *Blue Bird* a remarkably comfortable, commodious little daylight domeliner.

Though mechanically and in layout the three dome coaches and dome parlor observations were

45

Linen-finish post cards, typical of the 1950s, show the *Blue Bird* inside and out. (Author's Collection)

virtual replicas of the *Twin Zephyr's* cars, design touches inside gave them individual personalities. Most striking were the wall-size murals painted by Auriel Bessemer. Adorning the forward bulkhead of each dome, these canvases depicted aspects of life and commerce in the part of the Midwest through which the *Blue Bird* traveled. General responsibility for the interior decor was shared by John Harbeson, a Philadelphia-based industrial architect who had done other work for Budd, and Wabash's passenger and mechanical departments. Each dome coach had a different color scheme; unsurprisingly, the keynote color was blue.

It remained blue — even after 1964 when, thanks to merger, Wabash's dome fleet passed to Norfolk & Western. The three ex-*Blue Bird* dome coaches were refurbished in N&W's Roanoke Shops, then assigned to the Cincinnati–Norfolk *Powhatan Arrow*, where they were billed as the "only dome cars in regular service in the south." (This was true only assuming that the "regular service" stipulation disqualified the leased Northern Pacific dome sleepers that were a regular part of the winter-season consists of both the *City of Miami* and the *South Wind*.)

After N&W's daylight *Powhatan Arrow* was discontinued in 1969, the domes were shifted to the overnight *Pocahontas* on that same route. In its final years this train received a modest gussying-up, rather remarkable considering the era. "All equipment has been thoroughly modernized and redecorated," according to a brochure explaining the enhancements. "The *Pocahontas* gone modern is like taking a cruise ship on rails — but at much less cost." Services touted included "scenic dome car, cocktail lounge, dining car, private sleeping quarters, or an air-conditioned reclining seat coach." The train ran until the advent of Amtrak, which put the three ex-*Blue Bird* dome coaches (and the ex-*Blue Bird* Budd observation as well) on its roster.

The second largest single order for Budd short domes, surpassed only by the CB&Q-WP-D&RGW *Twin Zephyr/California Zephyr* order for 40 cars in 1945, was for Canadian Pacific's re-equipping of the Montreal and Toronto–Vancouver *Dominion* and creation of the all-new *Canadian* on those routes. As part of a 173-car order from Budd would come 36 "Scenic Domes": 18 dome sleeper-observation-lounges and 18 dome coach-buffet lounges.

The westbound *Canadian* wearing CP Rail garb at Medicine Hat, Alberta. (Steve Patterson)

Lights are on in the Skyline dome as the westbound *Canadian* pauses in Kenora, Ontario, in January of 1987. (Karl Zimmermann)

Skyline coffee shop menu covers showed the Skyline dome in various settings, including the Rockies. (Bob Schmidt Collection)

Canadian Pacific's Skyline and Park domes initially saw service on the *Canadian* and the *Dominion*. Note the raised beaver herald at the car ends. (Lawrence S. Williams: Peter Tilp Collection)

The now-famous Park-series observation cars, named for national and provincial parks in Canada, were built to the same plans as the *CZ* obs cars, with three double bedrooms, a drawing room, an under-dome cocktail bar, and a lounge in the observation end. Their kinship was apparent outside as well, though the CP cars lacked the *CZ's* distinctive rear-end Mars light, and narrow wine-red bands circled the Park cars at the letterboards and window belt rail while the *CZ* observations were adorned only by black lettering. All the *Canadian* and *Dominion* cars carried the CPR beaver crest in relief by the vestibule doors, an elegant touch. Car names were red edged in gold.

Like the *CZ* observations, the Park cars were Cadillacs. Though Budd domes routinely featured original art in their decor, the under-dome Mural Lounges in the Park cars became preeminent for this. Each of the 18 cars had a unique oil-on-canvas mural of the car's namesake park. Executed and signed by a member of the Royal Canadian Academy of Arts, the murals covered two walls — bulkhead and window. The artists were chosen by Robert W. Pilot, president of the Academy. For each car, the same artist provided an illuminated map of the park, which hung over the writing desk in the lounge area to the rear of the car.

In the Mural Lounges, which CP described as "intimate as an exclusive club," the bar fronts were hand-carved, hand-painted linoleum. The room was separated from the corridor by etched, edge-lighted glass.

CP's 18 midtrain Scenic Domes — which carried no individual names, but were generically called "Skyline" coffee-shop cars — provided dome space for coach passengers. Though they had coach seating in the long end rather than crew dormitories, these cars were kin to the *CZ* buffet lounges. Each consist, *Canadian* or *Dominion,* carried one of each type of dome, which admittedly didn't add up to a great deal of dome space when compared to the *CZ* or the *Empire Builder.* (Burlington's original formula, operative at the time of the *CZ* and *Twin Zephyr* orders, was one dome seat for every two revenue places. The *Canadian* fell far short of this, coming up at roughly one per five.)

The first dome delivered from CP's order arrived in July of 1954; with a new Budd sleeper, it went on a 10,000-mile transcontinental exhibition tour. The stainless-steel fleet grew as the months passed. When inaugurated in 1955, the new flagship, the *Canadian,* would have an almost pure Budd stainless-steel consist, though it drew from a pool of 22 fourteen-section heavyweight tourist sleepers rebuilt by the railroad and adorned with stainless-steel sheathing to match the Budd cars. A smart, dazzling train, the *Canadian* contrasted sharply with Canadian National's rather dowdy *Super Continental,* inaugurated simultaneously, which wouldn't get domes until the middle of the next decade.

Though CP's Scenic Domes are most closely associated with the *Canadian* — and rightly so, since they've continued uninterrupted in that service — the cars have had a variety of other assignments.

49

The low-profile domes that Budd built for the *Chessie* were unique in their raked appearance. The sleeper, seen here, was also unique in its room arrangement, shown opened made down for sleeping. (C&O Railway: C&O Historical Society Collection)

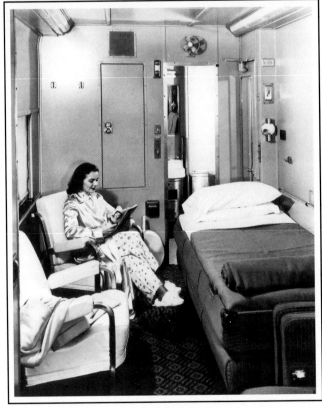

Initially both the Toronto and Montreal sections of the *Dominion* — the once-premier train that played second fiddle to the *Canadian* after the latter's inaugural — carried Skylines and Park cars in its mixed consist of heavyweights and Budd-built lightweights. That assignment, along with the *Canadian*, employed all the domes — for each train, seven consists for Montreal–Vancouver and two to protect the Toronto–Sudbury stub.

By the late fifties, the Toronto section of the *Dominion* alternately ran without the Skyline or Park car. Then, in the fall of 1960, the train changed its personality completely, losing its through sleepers, diner, and domes for the winter season — a practice that continued up until the *Dominion's* discontinuance in 1966. The domes freed up in the off-season appeared in various services out of Montreal, with the Park cars running as parlors.

These dome-obs cars ran on the Montreal–Quebec City *Frontenac* and *Viger* and the Montreal–Ottawa *Rideau*, and Skylines on the Montreal–St. John *Atlantic Limited.* Later, in the fall of 1965, a pair of new Montreal–Toronto trains — the eastbound *Le Chateau Champlain* and the westbound *Royal York*, both named for Canadian Pacific hotels in the destination cities — were touted as "Scenic Dome Stainless Steel Streamliners" and carried both Park and Skyline cars. Both trains left at 5 p.m. and arrived at 10:45 p.m.; seats could be reserved in advance in the "deluxe Dining Room car." This train ran for one season only.

Next beneficiary of the domes not needed for the *Canadian* were Montreal–Ottawa trains 233 and 234, beginning in 1966. The following season domes appeared on another pair, 232 and 235, and domes remained in service to Ottawa until the trains were axed in 1970. This left as the only CP domeliners the *Canadian* and the *Atlantic Limited* (which through the sixties had fallen into and out of this category).

A pair of CP's Skyline cars garnered considerable attention in August of 1974 when they were leased to

The *Chessie* dome observation-lounges ran briefly on the Detroit–Grand Rapids *Pere Marquette,* seen here in October, 1948, near St. Joseph, Michigan. (C&O Railway: C&O Historical Society Collection)

the Delaware & Hudson for the start-up of the New York City–Montreal *Adirondack,* a train officially if not apparently under Amtrak aegis. D&H splashed its name across the letterboards in blue and yellow, dubbed the cars Bluff Point (CP's No. 507) and Willsboro Point (No. 500) for prominent Lake Champlain locales, and served full meals aboard.

The Skylines' assignment was only temporary, lasting from the train's inception until the following spring. Then D&H's own diner-lounges — former Rio

Grande *Prospector* cars acquired in 1967 (along with Rio Grande baggage cars and coaches and four Santa Fe Alco PA's) to spruce up *Adirondack*-predecessor *Laurentian* — returned from refurbishing. (After a six-month hiatus, Amtrak began providing dome coaches from its own fleet, until Turboliners took over the *Adirondack* assignment on March 1, 1977.)

The Canadian's domes win the prize for longevity of assignment, hands down. A full 40 years after their delivery, they remained in the service for which they were acquired: plying Toronto–Vancouver on the *Canadian,* albeit on a different route. At the other extreme were six domes built by Budd for Chesapeake & Ohio in 1948. Far from lasting 40 years, they were cast off by C&O almost immediately — and never even entered the service for which they were ordered: the *Chessie,* the projected Washington–Cincinnati standard-bearer for Robert R. Young's postwar passenger rebirth on the C&O.

Hoping to set the pace for the entire industry, Young (who was then C&O's chairman) in 1944 and 1946 ordered a total of 351 passenger cars, with which he planned to modernize completely C&O's passenger operations. The vast majority of the cars were to come from Pullman-Standard, but the crème de la crème — the 46 cars for the ultra-luxury, daytime *Chessie* — would be Budd products. The *Chessie* was to be pulled by a trio of striking-looking (and, as it turned out, strikingly unsuccessful) steam turbine-electrics, built by C&O, Baldwin, and Westinghouse in 1947 and 1948 and quietly scrapped in 1950.

Plans changed radically over the long wait for the cars to be delivered by builders overextended by the postwar boom. Passenger business was off, and finances generally not good, so at the eleventh hour the *Chessie* was canceled before ever being inaugurated and the 46 Budd-built cars — enough for two 11-car consists and a spare train, plus two four-car connecting trains (Charlottesville–Newport News and Ashland–Louisville) — eventually dispersed. By the end of 1951, only four of the 46 cars remained C&O property (and only 130 of the grand total of 351 cars meant to transform the railroad's passenger service).

Two of the cars in each planned *Chessie* consist were domes: a private-room dome car to be run midtrain and the tail car, a dome coach-observation-lounge. Destined to be vagabonds and mavericks, the six were the only Budd short domes not conforming to the eventually classic pattern established by the *Twin Zephyr* of 1947. The *Chessie* domes were of a lower profile (15 feet 5¾ inches, about 4 inches shorter than the standard Budd short dome) because of Eastern clearances — and in particular the tunnels into Washington Union Station from the south — and were built with a combination of flat and curved glass. Furthermore, the side windows in the dome were forward-canted parallelograms, angular and raked, suggesting speed — a style never repeated by the builder.

Both types of *Chessie* dome were unusually configured. The dome observation had 20 coach seats forward, washrooms and a gift shop under the dome, and a lounge for 16 in the observation end. Here the seats were cleverly arranged in a single zig-zagging banquette, all facing out for excellent visibility.

The dome sleepers were even more singular — especially considering that the *Chessie* was to be a daytime train. Originally intended as the operations center for the *Chessie,* the cars as built provided six roomettes for train personnel; a communications center, from which music, announcements, and route information were to be piped to the coach seats, and day rooms (two doubles and one single, called "cabins") for passengers. The cars were subsequently rebuilt for sleeper service, leaving them with an unusual space configuration: three drawing rooms, five roomettes, and, under the dome, a spacious single bedroom, along with a porter's berth and conductor's room.

Because of the aspirations of the *Chessie* streamliner, the cars were unusually luxurious in their finish. The coach section of the dome-observation, for instance, had a photomural of Washington, D.C., on the bulkhead, and beneath that an enclosed wooden cabinet meant to contain a lending library. There was carpeting on the floor, venetian blinds at the windows, aircraftlike pockets in the seatbacks, and — on a room divider — a clock with a smart modern face.

The six *Chessie* domes were orphans from the beginning. For a time the three dome observations ran on the Detroit–Grand Rapids *Pere Marquette,* but in 1949 the cars headed west, sold to the D&RGW for use on the Denver–Salt Lake City *Royal Gorge.* Rio Grande felt obliged to run these observation cars midtrain (perhaps to facilitate combination with the *Prospector* west of Grand Junction) and thus added an ungainly diaphragm to the round end.

Apparently the sleeper domes were never in regular assignment on the C&O. They were sent to the Dwight Austin Company shops at Kent, Ohio, to be modified for overnight service, and returned in the fall of 1950. The railroad had planned that the domes would enter service in Pullman lease on trains 46 and 47, the *Sportsman,* on the Phoebus, Virginia (Old Point Comfort)–Detroit sleeper line, but they never did.

H. T. Askew, C&O's General Passenger Traffic Manager at the time of the cars' delivery, recalls that they were run on the *Sportsman* — but only on a trial basis. (The train was steam-powered at the time, and the cinders from the locomotive reportedly caked on the front dome windows.) C&O had planned to name them — Belle Isle Dome, Chamberlin Dome, and Hampton Roads Dome — but never did that either. They remained simply Nos. 1850–1852 during their brief, largely inactive lives on the C&O, which ended in December 1950 when the cars were sold to the Baltimore & Ohio.

B&O did give them names: Moonlight Dome, Starlight Dome, and Sunlight Dome. Beginning on December 20, the latter two operated in daily service on the Washington–Chicago *Capitol Limited,* while Moonlight Dome was carried in alternate directions each day by the Washington–Chicago *Shenandoah.*

Dome sleepers were never common. In addition to these three there were only Dream Cloud from the *Train of Tomorrow* and the fleet of 11 that Budd built for the *North Coast Limited* — plus the *CZ* and *Canadian* dome observation-lounges, which had sleeping space. But despite their unsettled beginnings, the C&O dome sleepers had a long and successful career on the B&O. After purchase by the Seaboard Coast Line in September 1969 for its *Florida Special,* the cars ran well into the Amtrak era, among the most-traveled and best-known of domes.

NORTH COAST LIMITED: DOMES IN THE LAND OF LEWIS AND CLARK

Way back on April 29, 1900, the Northern Pacific inaugurated the *North Coast Limited,* initially as a summer-only luxury train from St. Paul to Seattle. Just two years later Nos. 1 and 2, as it was then designated, proved popular enough to go into year-round service. In 1911 the train was extended to Chicago, running on the Chicago & North Western until 1918, when it was switched to the Burlington.

The *North Coast Limited* entered the streamliner era in 1948, when Pullman-Standard completed delivery of six sets of lightweight cars to modernize the train. The great bulk of these coaches, Pullmans, counter-diners, and lounges were owned by NP, though two joint operators — the Burlington and the Spokane, Portland & Seattle, which handled the train's Portland section from Pasco, Washington — accounted for a few.

For the next dozen years the *North Coast Limited's* consist and appearance were repeatedly altered and refined. In 1952 the train's exterior received from industrial designer Raymond Loewy an elegant two-tone green paint scheme. It was in this scheme, in 1954, that the ten dome coaches and ten dome sleepers were delivered from the Budd Company. (The train's schedule had been speeded up sufficiently since 1948 that now only five, not six, sets of equipment were needed to protect it.) The first dome entered service on August 16, and all were rolling by fall. Also in 1954, five flat-top sleepers were delivered from P-S.

These and the dome sleepers set a new trend, carrying only numbers, no name; existing sleepers then lost their names in conformity.

With the additional seating provided by the arrival of the dome coaches, chair-buffet lounges were withdrawn from the consist and rebuilt into "Lewis and Clark Traveller's Rest" lunch-counter-tavern cars. This new look was also the work of Raymond Loewy Associates (as were the interiors of the dome cars). The domes, four in each consist initially, were surely welcome on the *North Coast Limited,* which ran through some exceptionally beautiful country — particularly in Montana, where the NP followed the Lewis and Clark Trail.

The *North Coast Limited* survived until Amtrak buried it on May 1, 1971 — only to exhume it shortly thereafter as the *North Coast Hiawatha,* a compromise train that proved to have a limited future, but plenty of domes in the interim.

A NEW *BLUE BIRD* TAKES WING

By the time the new Wabash *Blue Bird,* a gleaming Budd-built domeliner, was christened at St. Louis Union Station on February 26, 1950, the heavyweight *Blue Bird* had already long been a fixture in the fierce St. Louis–Chicago passenger-train wars — as had running mate *Banner Blue,* which would eventually share the *Blue Bird's* dome largess. Sometimes called the "rainbow race," the color-coded competition among Wabash's "Blue" trains, Illinois Central's *Green Diamond,* and Alton's red-painted consists was intense. No doubt the Wabash got a leg up by offering the first domes between those cities — and the only ones, until Amtrak.

Wabash was coming from behind. The Alton (which became part of the Gulf, Mobile & Ohio in 1947) traditionally offered the most St. Louis–Chicago trains and carried the most passengers. Wabash had the high-speed route, but Decatur, Illinois, was the only significant population center along the way, while GM&O's line had many. And both the IC with its *Green Diamond* and Alton with its *Abraham Lincoln* and *Ann Rutledge* had entered the streamliner era in the mid-thirties.

"When other railroads serving the territory assigned streamline equipment and diesel power to their day trains operating in this service," said Wabash president Arthur K. Atkinson, "we felt it necessary to meet our competition with comparable or even superior equipment and service." This the Wabash did — eventually. The railroad's first brush with streamlining was the November 1947 inauguration of the Kansas City–St. Louis *City of Kansas City*, a seven-car consist outshopped by American Car & Foundry at St. Charles, Missouri.

Three years later came the *Blue Bird*, a spiffy little Domeliner. (And apparently the term "Domeliner" was coined by Leo Brown, advertising manager for the Wabash; in 1954 he formally gave Union Pacific permission to use it, and it was UP that would give the term its greatest prominence.) Just six cars long, the train was sleek, fluted stainless steel in the Budd tradition but also showed plenty of the obligatory blue: on skirting, on window panels, and on letterboards and numberboards, where car identities were inscribed in gold.

The identity of the train itself was proclaimed by an octagonal illuminated tailsign, which read "The Blue Bird" in flowing script, flanked by a small Wabash flag and a bird in flight. This tailsign was successor to a similar drumhead that had adorned the open observation platforms of standard parlor cars such as Helena Modjeska and Clara Morris, 1924 Pullman products that had served the train in its heavyweight days.

Well established as the *Blue Bird's* Chicago–St. Louis consort was the *Banner Blue*, operating the flip side of the *Blue Bird's* new morning-eastbound, afternoon-westbound schedule over the 286-mile route. (Dieselization had sped up the *Blue Bird* sufficiently to enable a single consist to turn and work both directions. The heavyweight *Blue Bird* had been an afternoon train both ways.) Though the *Banner Blue* was dieselized at the *Blue Bird's* streamlining and "doming," for years afterward it remained a substantially heavyweight, domeless train, with a schedule that required two consists to operate. In fact, though the *Blue Bird* began sharing its dome coaches with its running mate in the early sixties and later its Budd-built dome parlor-observation, the *Banner Blue* kept a heavyweight parlor-observation — City of Lafayette — as one of the three parlors needed to protect the service long after most similar cars had been consigned to scrap.

The Wabash dome shuffle began early in the *Blue Bird's* career, in August 1952, when Pullman-Standard delivered a second dome parlor car for the train, freeing one of the dome coaches for assignment to the railroad's Kansas City–St. Louis streamliner *City of Kansas City*. This P-S parlor, with the distinctive "Blue Bird Room" (a first-class lounge, also available for private gatherings) under the dome, would end up fifteen years later as the train's one and only dome.

Wabash was merged into the Norfolk & Western in October of 1964; that, plus the general decline of passenger railroading in the sixties, soon led to dome attrition on the *Blue Bird*. By mid-decade that train and the *Banner Blue* each had a dome coach, and the *Blue Bird* the P-S dome parlor. The *Banner Blue's* parlor car typically would be either a 1947 ACF observation built for the *City of Kansas City*, the Budd dome parlor-observation from the *Blue Bird*, or the City of Lafayette.

Then, in the fall of 1966, the dome coaches were reassigned to N&W's *Powhatan Arrow*; that left the *Banner* domeless once again, and the *Bird* with just the P-S dome parlor. A year later the *Blue Bird* lost its last dome and the *Banner Blue* its life.

By the time the *Blue Bird* fluttered into oblivion at Amtrak's creation, it had been transformed to the unimposing-sounding *City of Decatur*, shorn not only of its domes but also of the southern 113 miles of its traditional route.

THE *CANADIAN*: REMARKABLE SURVIVOR

On April 24, 1955, Canada entered the streamliner era in a big way, with both Canadian National and Canadian Pacific fielding new lightweight trains. These competing streamliners, CN's *Super Continental* and CP's *Canadian*, had a lot more in common than a birthday. Both offered separate sections to serve Toronto and Montreal, combining in northern Ontario (Sudbury on the CP and Capreol on the CN) for the rest of the journey to Vancouver. Both were new trains, supplementing rather than replacing existing services. Both operated on substantially accelerated schedules.

What they didn't have in common was domes. Here CP stood alone — and this was emblematic of the fact that the gleaming *Canadian* was a tonier train than the *Super Continental*, right from the beginning. Most of the CN train's consist was new, drawn from a 359-car order from Pullman-Standard and Canadian Car & Foundry delivered in 1954. But there were only two or three sleepers as opposed to the Canadian's six and a half (counting the Park car), and the full diner ran only Toronto–Vancouver, with a Montreal–Winnipeg dinette car serving the needs of the other section.

If the *California Zephyr* was (as its publicists claimed) "the most talked-about train in America," surely the look-alike *Canadian* has been the most talked-about train in Canada. Finding their own exclusives and superlatives, CP's ad men wrote at the *Canadian's* inaugural of "Canada's only dome cars" and "the longest dome ride in the world."

An NP Pullman dome is at the front of the northbound *City of Miami* consist leaving Champaign, Illinois, in October 1959. (J. Parker Lamb)

The Chicago-bound *Blue Bird* speeds across central Illinois cornfields near Mansfield on a warm July day in 1958. A heavyweight Pullman parlor car amplifies the seating space available in the parlor section of the observation car. (J. Parker Lamb)

With a baggage car, not a round-end observation car, bringing up the rear, the St. Louis-bound *Blue Bird* arriving Decatur, Illinois, at dusk in 1959 is a far less imposing-looking train than had been inaugurated just nine years earlier. The dome count was halved, with a Pullman-Standard dome parlor car substituting for the Budd dome observation-parlor. (J. Parker Lamb)

In something of a public-relations coup, Canadian Pacific and the Budd Company were tied into a promotion involving *Vogue* magazine and 112 stores in the United States and Canada. The theme was "A Vacation Trip Across Canada," which filled much of the April 15, 1955, issue of *Vogue* with the trip itself and the appropriate wardrobe for a female passenger.

Inaugural festivities centered equally in Montreal, Toronto, and Vancouver. After the appropriate hoopla of christenings and introductions (which CN had carried on the day before) Nos. 1 and 2, the all-new *Canadian,* were off and running. In its original timing, No. 1 left Montreal at 1 p.m., while No. 11 left Toronto at 4:15 p.m. They rendezvoused at Sudbury late that evening, then were off across the Canadian Shield.

The next morning brought a spectacular run along the north shore of Lake Superior, and the afternoon an immersion in the vastness of the prairie — a sea of wheat over which grain elevators stood watch like lighthouses. By the afternoon of the third day the Rockies hove into view, and the train called at Banff and Lake Louise. The Spiral Tunnels were negotiated before night fell on some of the continent's most famous scenery. At 9:10 the next morning the *Canadian* pulled into Vancouver — where passengers could make connections with one of Canadian Pacific Steamship Lines' Princess fleet in "Triangle Service" to Victoria (on Vancouver Island) and Seattle.

The *Canadian:* three nights, 71 hours, 2881 miles. Two domes, elegant diners named for famous rooms

The *Canadian,* looking smart in VIA blue, runs along the Bow River in Alberta. (Roger Cook)

in Canadian Pacific hotels, sleeping accommodations that included sections, roomettes, bedrooms, compartments, and drawing rooms. A sweep of country from the farmlands of Quebec through the rock-ribbed Shield to lush prairie through mountains to the Pacific.

All this was a combination that, happily, has thus far proven too good to die. With a $200 million re-furbishing of *Canadian* equipment, including conversion to head-end power, this beautiful domeliner continues to roll undimmed — albeit on a different route — through the 1990s.

4

Pullman-Standard
Not a Curve in Sight

Baltimore & Ohio was already something of a veteran dome operator by December 1950 when it took possession of the three dome sleepers Budd had built for the stillborn *Chessie*. Back on May 5, 1949, B&O had christened its new overnight Baltimore–Chicago all-coach *Columbian,* and both of the all-Pullman-Standard consists contained a Strata-Dome coach. Named High Dome (No. 5500) and Sky Dome No. 5501), they were the first P-S domes sold to a railroad. Only the domes of *Train of Tomorrow* were earlier.

The *Columbian's* two domes — and the even dozen cars cut from similar cloth and delivered in the next few years to Santa Fe, Missouri Pacific, Texas & Pacific, and Wabash — were intriguingly individualistic. All 137 of Budd's "short domes" (except the *Chessie* cars) were basically the same vehicle adapted to various functions and individually ornamented — a tried-and-true design so well accepted that it would have been foolish to consider major modifications. On the other hand, Pullman-Standard managed five relatively different designs in its 18 short domes, all fabricated of flat glass, which became its signature cars.

The dome areas aboard Pullman-Standard's B&O cars were distinctive. A large panel on the front bulkhead held a speedometer, altimeter, barometer, and clock. Below it, a speaker for the radio and public-address system — *de rigueur* during that era for any new train with cachet — showed a grill neatly adorned with a large "B&O." Moderne-style paired metal strips ran up the bulkhead and across the ceiling. The 24 dome seats had low backs for better visibility. In deference to the more cramped clearances in the East — and B&O touted its *Columbian* as the "first

Strata-Dome train built for any Eastern railroad," which was almost true (the *Chessie* cars were earlier) — the dome projected just 21 inches above normal roof height, as opposed to 28 inches for the standard Budd short domes and subsequent P-S domes. (B&O's P-S cars stood just 15 feet 3 inches tall, making them more than 2 inches lower than their ex-C&O Budd fleetmates.)

Downstairs in the *Columbian* domes were 18 coach seats forward and 24 aft. Below the dome were two step-down lounging areas, one seating 11 and the other six. Rather than being completely enclosed by full walls, these areas had waist-high railed partitions and were open above to the passageway through the car and the main seating area to the rear. This open expanse of interior space would have been impossible in a Budd dome, since it required elimination of one of the dome-end bulkheads. The bulkheads were crucial stress-bearing components in Budd's Shotwelded-stainless-steel design, picking up the redistributed stress normally borne by an unbroken roof line in flat-top cars. Pullman-Standard's carbon-steel cars were heavier, but their interior design was more flexible because only the underbody and side walls below the windows were structurally integral.

The Strata-Domes were just a few years old when, in 1952, B&O had a new wrinkle for its customers. The *Capitol Limited* and *Columbian* were overnight trains, so passengers had precious little daylight in which to view scenery through dome windows. Seizing the only apparent remedy, B&O added lights to its five-car dome fleet (which included the three Budd-built dome sleepers bought from C&O). Groups of four floodlights were placed just forward of the domes and directed off

58

Pullman-Standard coach High Dome, shown getting a bath (Baltimore & Ohio: Gary Schlerf Collection)

Above the speaker grill in Pullman-Standard's B&O domes were clock, speedometer, barometer, and altimeter. (Baltimore & Ohio: Gary Schlerf Collection)

Floodlights for night viewing, seen here aboard P-S dome No. 5550 — High Dome, though the name was gone by the time this 1960s photo was taken — were a unique feature of the B&O domes. The lights were introduced in 1952. (Peter Tilp Collection)

to the right, at angles of 60, 70, 80, and 85 degrees from the centerline of the train. Clear 250-watt locomotive headlights were used.

These lights produced what *Railway Age* described as a "diffused beam, somewhat stronger than bright moonlight." So as not to alarm the populace, the lights were turned off when the train passed through cities and towns. Icebreakers were later added to the roof to protect both dome and lights.

Late in their B&O careers, in the era of cutbacks, consolidations, and economies, Nos. 5500 and 5501 (which had lost their names in 1965) were significantly reconfigured on a shoestring for a new function. In November 1967, No. 5500 received a food-bar kitchen and serving area under the dome, where the two lounges, or "family areas," had been. Called the "Iron Horse Tavern," this small facility dispensed sandwiches, snacks, and beverages. No. 5501 was similarly modified in February 1968.

The Pullman-Standard domes would wear various liveries during their lifetimes, beginning with B&O's fine blue and gray scheme with yellow striping and silver trucks. In the 1960s the P-S domes, like most B&O passenger cars, were repainted in partner C&O's blue, gray, and yellow dress. And in 1969 No. 5501 wore powder blue with a silver roof — the colors of Ross Rowland's New York City–Ogden, Utah, *Golden Spike Centennial Limited*. In 1970 B&O/C&O applied a final scheme, one designed by William Howes, the roads' director of passenger services, who later characterized the livery he created as "a dud."

The next Pullman-Standard domes to appear after B&O's were the six "Pleasure Domes" for the Chicago–Los Angeles *Super Chief,* Santa Fe's all-Pullman flagship. These cars, which entered service in December 1950, owe a considerable design debt to Moon Glow, the *Train of Tomorrow's* observation lounge, sharing virtually the same floor plan. Santa Fe's cars had two unique features, however: the Turquoise Room, which was the first private dining room aboard a train; and parlor-car-style revolving seats in the dome.

The Turquoise Room, in the short end of the car, always coupled to the diner, could seat 12, and was available for private luncheon, cocktail, or dinner parties. The room could be booked with the steward or through traffic representatives in advance of travel. When not reserved for a private party, it was used as

The circle of dome-car use on B&O was closed by the commemorative last run of the *Capitol Limited*, seen here on May 1, 1971 — the day Amtrak was born. Amtrak would eventually bring back the *Capitol Limited*, and even stock it with domes for a time. (Herbert H. Harwood: William F. Howes, Jr., Collection)

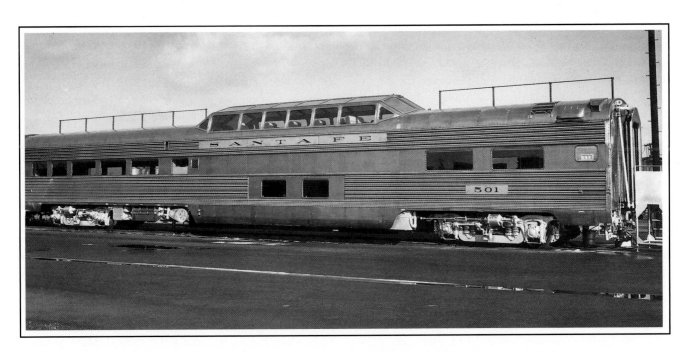

Santa Fe's "Pleasure Domes" for the *Super Chief* were unique cars, with parlor-style swivel chair in the dome and private dining in the Turquoise Room. (Santa Fe Railway)

Pullman-Standard *Eagle* coach No. 200 was owned by Texas & Pacific. (Pullman-Standard: Joseph M. Welsh Collection)

overflow seating for the diner. The room's decorative keynote was a reproduction of a silver-accented Indian turquoise medallion, displayed in a shadow box on the forward wall. Under the dome was a cozy cocktail room, and forward was a large lounge.

The dome seating was certainly unusual. Nearly 200 short domes were built — by Budd, Pullman-Standard, and, later, American Car & Foundry — and every one but Santa Fe's six "Pleasure Domes" and UP's 11 dome diners (including the *Train of Tomorrow* car) originally had coach-style seating for 24. Instead, these *Super Chief* cars featured eight revolving parlor chairs in the center of the dome area. Flanking them front and back were coach-style double seats — the forward ones facing forward, the rearward ones rearward. The oversized parlor chairs were particularly comfortable and could be pivoted freely for ideal viewing angles. On the negative side, they reduced the dome's seating capacity to 16, only two-thirds of the standard, which was a bit skimpy for an entire train, even an all-Pullman one with its relatively shorter passenger list. Still, the Pleasure Domes were surely among the most distinctive and luxurious cars ever built.

Originally these cars were to be named. Names, in fact, were actually chosen — Plaza Acoma, Plaza Laguna, Plaza Lamy, Plaza Santa Fe, Plaza Taos, and Plaza Zuni — but for whatever reason the domes lived out their Santa Fe and subsequent Amtrak careers in the anonymity of numbers, 500 through 505. (Subsequently, in private ownership, some of these names have been applied.)

In 1957, as part of Santa Fe's general "buffing up" of its flagship *Super Chief,* the Pleasure Domes received substantial cosmetic renovation. New furniture was added to the main lounge, as well as a lowered ceiling with indirect lighting. The dome area and Turquoise room were redecorated as well; the latter was paneled in vertical wooden lathing, with the turquoise medallion remaining the decorative accent.

In August 1952 Pullman-Standard delivered three "Planetarium Dome" coaches to Missouri Pacific and one each to subsidiaries Texas & Pacific and International-Great Northern for service from St. Louis on the *South Texas Eagle* and *West Texas Eagle.* These cars — which joined the three Budd products already in the Mopac fleet, acquired in 1948 for the *Colorado Eagle* — offered seating for 83: 24 in the dome, 42 in coach seats on the main level, and 17 in the dropped area under the dome, which was open to the passageway and to the rear main-level section, as in the B&O coach domes.

Also in August 1952 came a single P-S dome parlor to join the consist of Wabash's *Blue Bird.* Tucked under its dome was the "Blue Bird Room," available like the Turquoise Room for private parties. When not in demand for such exclusive gatherings, the room was used as a first-class lounge; dining tables were designed to be easily collapsed and removed. When this car was added to the train, one of its Budd dome coaches was transferred to the Kansas City–St. Louis *City of Kansas City,* becoming the second dome to operate in the Missouri River Valley (the *Colorado Eagle* was the first, in 1948).

Wabash added a single additional dome to its roster for *Blue Bird* service in 1952 — a parlor car from Pullman-Standard. The paint scheme was designed to blend with the train's stainless-steel cars from Budd. (Pullman-Standard: Joe Welsh Collection)

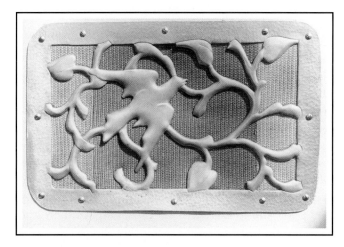

The speaker grille in the dome of the Wabash's P-S car carried a graceful *Blue Bird* design. (Roger Cook)

Adding the Pullman-Standard dome to the all-Budd *Blue Bird* consist might have seemed a curious move on the part of Wabash. Reportedly, however, parlor-car patronage on the Chicago–St. Louis domeliner had exceeded expectations, and P-S was in a better position than Budd to deliver an additional dome parlor on short notice. By coordinating its order with the dome lot to be built for Missouri Pacific (and subsidiaries), Wabash was able to secure a single extra dome without the expense normally associated with a single-car order.

The Mopac and Wabash cars were the last of the P-S flat-glass short-dome fleet begun with the *Train of Tomorrow*. Due from P-S later that year, in December, were ten Super Domes for the Milwaukee Road. They would enter service January 1, 1953, on the *Hiawathas*. Six years later, in December 1958, Pullman-Standard would deliver to Union Pacific and Wabash the last domes ever built — six chair cars, manufactured to American Car & Foundry plans, for the City of St. Louis. Pullman-Standard all-time, all-styles dome total: 34.

B&O'S *COLUMBIAN, CAPITOL,* AND *SHENANDOAH* BRING DOMES TO THE EAST

The dome car was essentially a Western phenomenon — for one compelling reason, plus some subsidiary ones, including the often spectacular nature of Western scenery. Basically, however, these over-height cars simply didn't fit within the more constrained clearances in the East.

For this reason, the Baltimore & Ohio was the only Eastern road among the original dome-car operators (leaving aside a brief stint on the Pere Marquette by the dome observations that Chesapeake & Ohio had built for the *Chessie* streamliner that never ran).

The *Super Chief's* dome car in Apache Canyon, New Mexico (Arthur Riordan: Peter Tilp Collection)

B&O's first domeliner was the *Columbian*, a new overnight Washington–Chicago streamliner inaugurated in May 1949 to replace a heavyweight train of the same name that had begun life as a New York–Washington service. (Early publicity brochures always referred to the "New Columbian," as if the adjective was formally part of the train's name, but timetables consistently listed the train simply as the *Columbian*.) The twin consists needed to protect the *Columbian* were built entirely by Pullman-Standard; though coaches-only, they were very spiffy indeed.

In addition to a Strata-Dome chair car — High Dome or Sky Dome — each consist included a baggage-dormitory-coffee shop car, a diner, a tavern-observation, and four 56-seat chair cars. The train offered stewardess-nurse service; radio, wire-recorded music, and public-address announcements throughout the consist; and Venetian blinds at the windows.

Though this coach streamliner was originally planned as a daylight train between Baltimore–Washington and Chicago, it was moved to an overnight schedule before inaugural — thus becoming in effect a running mate of the all-Pullman *Capitol Limited*, which operated between Chicago and Washington on a nearly identical schedule. (Both the *Capitol* and *Columbian* carried through cars for Jersey City, operating via B&O-Reading-Jersey Central.)

The illustrious *Capitol* was the B&O's flagship, and it didn't lag too far behind the *Columbian* in achieving domeliner status. In December of 1950, after B&O acquired from C&O the trio of dome sleepers built by Budd for the *Chessie*, two of the cars went on the *Capitol*. The third offered every-other-day service (for Pullman passengers only) on the *Shenandoah*, a Washington–Chicago train with a later schedule and lesser pretensions. The domes on the *Capitol* were the final step in a postwar upgrade that included new sleepers from Pullman-Standard and modernized club-lounge and observation cars.

The *Capitol Limited* had been born in 1923 as B&O's all-Pullman answer to the *20th Century Limited* and *Broadway Limited*, the all-Pullman flyers of the New York Central and Pennsylvania Railroad, B&O's more powerful rivals to the north. In spite of the excellence of its cuisine and the friendliness of its service, the *Capitol* never did quite acquire the cachet of the *Broadway* or,

Missouri Pacific originally applied a complex and elegant color scheme to its domes (John S. Ingles)

In 1969, for the *Golden Spike Centennial Limited,* B&O's No. 5501, previously Sky Dome, was painted in powder blue livery and lettered "American Railroads" to match the rest of the train. After the car returned to B&O service, it kept its light blue dress for a time, with B&O capitol emblems added at the car ends. (Bob Johnston)

from C+O-B+O glass-topped
STRATADOME CARS - a
unique travel experience

— C+O-B+O supports
President Lyndon B. Johnson's
"Let's sell the World on
Discovering America"

The Strata Dome was still a big selling point for "The Affiliated Chesapeake & Ohio Railway and Baltimore & Ohio Railroad," with Paul Reistrup as Director of Passenger Services, when they issued their fall 1966 timetable with this ad on the back cover. (Author's Collection)

particularly, the *Century*. But one thing it had that the other two trains never could was dome cars.

B&O's domes entered service at a time when the railroad remained bullish on passenger trains, but within a few years retrenchment and consolidation of services would replace expansion and re-equipping as the order of the day. The first negative change — the combination of the *Columbian* and the Baltimore–Detroit *Ambassador* east of Willard, Ohio — left the domes unaffected, as did the second: the consolidation

of the *Capitol* with the *Columbian* west of Willard, which occurred in 1958.

Then, after the 1961 summer season, the *Capitol*, *Columbian*, and *Ambassador* were all consolidated, though they retained their own names and numbers in the public timetables. And both the *Capitol* and the *Columbian* kept their domes. But then in April 1964 the *Columbian* vanished — name, number, and all — and its domes were shifted to the *Capitol*. This spelled the end in B&O service for the ex-C&O dome sleepers, done in

"Time is pleasure aboard the Super Chief," according to this brochure. (Bob Schmidt Collection)

by their relatively low sleeping capacity and nonstandard room configurations, not easily understood (or sold) by interline agents.

A few years later the P-S cars had their underdome areas converted to provide a primitive food service — meeting a need that surfaced when the *Capitol's* twin-unit diners (ex-New York Central cars acquired to meet the expanded needs of the consolidated train) were replaced in October 1967 with single cars. A year later the domes were shifted over to provide the only food service on the Cincinnati–Detroit *Cincinnatian*. The next summer they were back on the *Capitol*, but they ended their careers on a newly minted Washington–Akron *Shenandoah*, part of yet another service restructuring aimed at stemming losses. (No. 5500's career had been interrupted in its twilight when, on December 25, 1969, it was badly damaged in

a derailment at Lucas, Pennsylvania, on the Pittsburgh & Lake Erie. Not until November 1970 did the crippled car make it into the *Shenandoah* consist.)

But on the eve of Amtrak the two Pullman-Standard domes had one last hurrah, running back-to-back on the last eastbound *Capitol Limited* — the last that B&O would ever run, at any rate. For ten years later Amtrak would revive the train and the name — and five years after that, truly déjà vu, add domes.

THE *SUPER CHIEF* AND ITS "PLEASURE DOME"

For Santa Fe's illustrious *Super Chief,* a dome car was just icing on the cake.

Among the most famous trains ever, the always-Pullman-only *Super Chief* began its career in 1936 as a

The Turquoise Room medallion shines through the window of the Pleasure Dome car. (Roger E. Puta, Melvern Finzer Collection)

temporarily heavyweight train — albeit dieselized and blazingly fast. The following year came the first Budd-built lightweight version — certainly one of the most beautiful trains ever, with its elegant interiors featuring Indian art and Flexwood Veneers of rare woods. (Flexwood Veneer was a thin layer of real wood mounted on a muslin backing.)

Initially a single trainset offering weekly service in each direction, the *Super* quickly was joined by a second, slightly less elegant consist, allowing twice-weekly service. In 1946, with the train's first postwar re-equipping, this was increased to every other day. Not until 1948, when the train received another complete re-equipping, was its frequency upped to daily.

In 1950 and 1951 the train was yet again almost completely re-equipped — for the third time in six years — and this version included the Pleasure Domes, as well as affiliated diners, and sleeping cars.

The *Super Chief* mystique had many wellsprings, not the least of which was the cachet of the movie stars and other celebrities who rode its cars in the pre-jet era. Splendid Fred Harvey meals played a part, as

did the way the railroad integrated Native American culture into its personality. And after the demise of the Milwaukee Road's *Olympian Hiawatha,* the only Chicago–West Coast streamliners operated by a single railroad were Santa Fe's — and such a railroad, where stylishness, speed, and superb maintenance have always been the norm.

After the introduction of the Pleasure Dome, and the Turquoise Room that was very much a part of its distinctiveness, both became prominent features in the Santa Fe's vigorous promotion of the train. For the full two decades from that 1951 re-equipping right up until Amtrak's ascension in 1971, the *Super Chief* remained almost fully intact (though it lost its observation car in 1958, when the practice began of combining the all-Pullman *Super* with the all-coach *El Capitan* for the off-season). But the Pleasure Dome was always there.

The indisputable evidence of the *Super Chief's* staying power was that Amtrak at its creation swallowed the train whole, Pleasure Domes, diners, and all — and kept it essentially intact for years, even after Santa Fe,

The *Texas Eagle* pulls into the station at Austin, Texas, on a warm August afternoon in 1964.
(J. Parker Lamb)

not best pleased by deteriorating service standards, in 1974 withdrew the right to use the illustrious name "Super Chief."

A FLIGHT OF *EAGLES*

Early in the streamliner era, many Western railroads coined evocative names for their lightweight fleets. Burlington had its *Zephyrs,* Rock Island its *Rockets,* Milwaukee its *Hiawathas,* Southern Pacific its *Daylights.* On Union Pacific there were "City" trains. And on the Missouri Pacific there were *Eagles.*

Missouri Pacific's first streamliner entered service on March 10, 1940, between Omaha and St. Louis, via Kansas City, with a pair of six-car consists styled by Raymond Loewy. Initially simply called *The Eagle,* these pocket streamliners, powered by slant-nosed Electro-

Motive Division E3s, introduced the lovely blue and gray color scheme that would subsequently dress the entire *Eagle* fleet. As more *Eagles* were fledged, this pioneer train came to be called the *Missouri River Eagle* to distinguish it from the new arrivals.

The first of these was the St. Louis–Denver *Colorado Eagle,* which on June 21, 1942, replaced the heavyweight *Scenic Limited* on that route. And this train would become the first dome-carrying *Eagle* as well, as part of the major postwar re-equipping of the road's passenger services that would bring still more *Eagles* into the Mopac nest.

The railroad's first streamliners had in fact put up some gaudy numbers. It took the *Missouri River Eagle* just two years and eight months to generate net income of $1,137,727 and thus earn back its cost. That must have looked good to management — at least until the *Colorado Eagle* covered its cost of $1,467,663 much faster, in an incredible 290 days.

By August of 1948, Missouri Pacific and subsidiary Texas & Pacific had ordered 134 lightweight cars from Budd, Pullman-Standard, and ACF. In the Budd portion of that order were the three Planetarium Domes (all Mopac) that earlier that summer had made the *Colorado Eagle* Missouri Pacific's first domeliner — and among the first on any railroad, for that matter. In all, ten of the 134 new cars were earmarked for upgrading the prewar *Colorado Eagle*. Other initial allocations included 39 cars for the St. Louis–Ft. Worth/El Paso *West Texas Eagle*, Nos. 1 and 2, and 30 cars for the St. Louis–San Antonio *South Texas Eagle*, Nos. 21 and 22. These trains — which soon were simply called the *Texas Eagles* and after September 1961, when they began to run combined between St. Louis and Texarkana, the *Texas Eagle* (no ess) — were inaugurated in 1948, replacing sections of the *Sunshine Special*, which had been the road's premier train. The *Texas Eagles* became domeliners in 1952 with the delivery of the five Pullman-Standard Planetarium Domes.

Though it qualified as an early entry into the dome sweepstakes, the *Colorado Eagle* ran mostly at night, leaving St. Louis and Denver around 4 p.m. and arriving Denver about 10 a.m. and St. Louis about noon (the time change accounting for the difference). Still, the two-hour-plus run at the route's western end — between Pueblo, Colorado, and Denver, on the rails of the Denver & Rio Grande Western — offered some fine mountain scenery off to the west and, except on the year's shortest days, was largely sunlit. (This 120-mile stretch of track hosted some other interesting dome cars in addition to the *Colorado Eagle's*. Ex-Chesapeake & Ohio domes ran on D&RGW's *Royal Gorge*, and the *Denver Zephyr's* "Chuck Wagon" Vista-Dome, among the through cars that continued on from Denver to Colorado Springs, covered the route's northernmost 45 miles.)

Compared to the West's grandest domeliners — the *CZ*, the UP's "City" trains, the *Super Chief* — the *Colorado Eagle* was a modest, friendly, workaday train featuring a diner-lounge, sleepers, and coaches. The *Texas Eagles* were cut from similarly humble cloth, generally carrying diner-lounges as the only "non-revenue" cars.

So the quaintly named "Planetarium Domes" were the *Eagles'* main claim to luxe. Once the five P-S cars were delivered, eight dome coaches in toto proved enough to stock the *Missouri River Eagle* as well as the *Colorado Eagle* and *Texas Eagles*, and the cars ran in all these services until the erosion of passenger service began in the middle sixties.

In 1964 the *Colorado Eagle* lost not only its dome but also its sleepers and diner-lounge — even its name. (Two years later it was discontinued entirely.) Also in 1964, the two domes running on the by-then-combined *Texas Eagle* were cut to one (the St. Louis–San Antonio car was retained), with the released cars going on newly designated Nos. 21 and 22 between New Orleans and Ft. Worth, the *Louisiana Eagle* route.

Then in 1967 Missouri Pacific withdrew all its domes and sold six — the three Budds and three of the five Pullman-Standards — to the Illinois Central.

By this time the once-proud *Eagle* fleet was largely grounded. When Amtrak arrived, all that was left to reject was the *Missouri River Eagle*, an anonymous St. Louis–Kansas City running mate, and a truncated, nameless remnant of the *Texas Eagle* — sans domes, sans diner-lounges, sans sleepers, sans almost everything.

The Full-Length Domes
Was Bigger Better?

There's no doubt they were impressive, the 30 full-length domes delivered by two builders, Pullman-Standard and Budd, for three Western lines — Milwaukee Road, Santa Fe, and Great Northern. Behemoths of the rails, these cars had such substantial passenger capacity — seating as many as 109, in the case of GN's — that the price tag, in the neighborhood of $325,000, could be justified, even though the seats were all "nonrevenue." And Southern Pacific's seven three-quarter-length, home-built dome lounges were only slightly less overwhelming.

Milwaukee's ten Super Domes, built by Pullman-Standard, became the first of their type when delivered in the last two months of 1952 — six for assignment to the Chicago–Seattle–Tacoma *Olympian Hiawatha* and two each for the Chicago–Twin Cities *Morning* and *Afternoon Hiawathas*. These cars, which marked the initial use of curved glass in Pullman-Standard domes, had 68 coach-style seats upstairs (in 30 pairs, plus four single seats at each end to accommodate open headroom above the corridor) and a 28-seat cafe below. Like the Budd-built full-lengths to follow, these enormous and potentially top-heavy cars rode on special six-wheel trucks with huge outboard springs to control body roll.

The glass area was so substantial — 625 square feet — that air conditioning of 16-ton capacity was required to keep the car cool. Powering this, and meeting the car's other electrical needs as well, was a 70-h.p. diesel generator. Air conditioners and generator, along with water and fuel tanks, were carried over the trucks, within the carbody, carefully placed to assure stability. Since the floor was dropped between the trucks, none of this equipment could be positioned under the car.

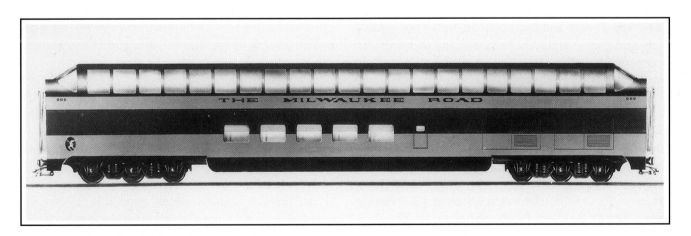

This artist's rendering whetted the appetite for what Milwaukee Road called "America's first all-dome railroad lounge cars." (Milwaukee Road Collection: Milwaukee Public Library)

The Super Dome's lower-level lounge for snacks and beverages seated 28. (Milwaukee Road Collection: Milwaukee Public Library)

The cars were undeniably imposing, 85 feet of all-welded girder-type construction, 112 tons of car. (Curiously, in spite of all the other superlatives, the Super Domes stood only 15 feet 6 inches tall, making them a full 4 inches lower, for instance, than the Budd domes, both short and full-length.) Originally the cars were dressed in the Milwaukee Road's traditional colors — Harvest Orange and Royal Maroon, with black under-body and roof — and were badged at one end with the smart, Art Deco "Hiawatha" emblem, an angular Indian warrior in flight across an oval field. Under the windows, in script, was written "Super Dome." This name had been chosen through a contest among employees; B. H. Perlick, head of the tie bureau in Chicago, received $150 for his winning suggestion. Runners-up, who received lesser prizes, suggested "Master Dome," "Panorama Dome," and "Ultra Dome" (a name which Princess Tours in Alaska would adopt in 1988 for its fleet of rebuilt Southern Pacific commute cars).

Inside, the under-dome cafe lounge was hand-somely appointed — and "the place to get acquainted, listen to the radio and enjoy a beverage," according to an inaugural publicity brochure on the cars. (In the *Olympian Hi's* under-dome cafe-lounges, soups, sand-wiches, and cold snacks were served in addition to bev-erages.) At one end, above a large curved settee, an illu-minated full-color photo mural behind cross-hatched mullions created the effect of a picture window. Seating was at two booths for five, three booths for four, and three tables for two. Gold-tinted mirrors etched with Indian designs of the Great Lakes and Plains regions adorned the pier panels between windows.

Though promoted as "perfectly planned in every detail," the dome area itself was most notable for its sheer size. "The huge windows — each pane is over three feet wide by five feet high — are especially con-structed," explained the inaugural brochure, touting this vastness and explaining how its inherent chal-lenges were met and shortcomings were minimized. "First, there is a quarter-inch outside layer of tem-pered plate glass. Then a sealed air space that prevents fogging and insulates against heat and cold. Finally, a three-eighth inch layer of laminated safety glass. These windows are actually as strong as a steel roof."

The Super Domes were featured in a 1956 brochure. (Jim Scribbins Collection)

The *Olympian Hiawatha*, its Super Dome, and even the box-cab electric motive power all wear Overland Route yellow in this June 1958 view at Seattle's Union Station. The tower at the far left is King Street Station, where the domes of Great Northern's *Empire Builder* and Northern Pacific's *North Coast Limited* arrived. The motor is running around its train to continue on for the one-hour, 38-mile run to Tacoma, where the train terminated. (Fred Matthews)

73

Santa Fe bought 14 Big Domes from Budd. No. 507 was in the first batch of eight, for the *El Capitan* and the *Chicagoan/Kansas Cityan*. (Santa Fe Railway)

In addition to 57 angled sightseeing seats forward, the upper level of the Big Domes offered this 18-seat club lounge area to the rear. (Santa Fe Railway)

Like Santa Fe's Big Domes, the *Empire Builder's* Great Domes were built by Budd; they were, in fact, virtually identical to the *El Cap* and *Chicagoan/Kansas Cityan* cars. (Great Northern: *Trains* Magazine Collection)

The commentary then deals with the great bugaboo of dome comfort: temperature. "The outer glass in all windows is of a special type with a slightly greenish tint," the explanation runs. "This not only reduces glare but filters out a portion of the heat.

"Of course, no clear glass can completely bar the radiant warmth of the sun. That's where air conditioning comes in. The Super Dome has its own system with a capacity great enough to cool three average size homes. Special 'solar disks' mounted on the roof measure the intensity of the sunshine and thermostatically regulate the air conditioning output to offset the heat of the sun." These expedients were typical of dome cars of other builders and other lines as well, and they were not always one hundred percent effective.

The Super Domes were unique in at least one way other than size: They were the only *Hiawatha* equipment other than sleeping cars not built by the railroad in its own shops. They were delivered by Pullman-Standard beginning in late November and were immediately sent out on the road for clearance checks at tight spots and crew briefings. On December 4 single cars were exhibited for railroad officials and the press at Chicago, Milwaukee, St. Paul, Minneapolis, and Seattle. Then over the next week six Super Domes were in public exhibition at on-line cities, staffed by representatives from the public relations and passenger traffic departments.

On December 6 the remaining four cars, joined by some flat-top equipment, ran two special trains between Chicago and Rondout, Illinois (32 miles to the northwest). On board were 900 passenger-department employees from Eastern and Southern roads. With the Pullman Company providing trip and berth passes, they came from as far away as Toronto, Boston, New York, Atlanta, and New Orleans to learn about these unexampled new full-length domes — and thus, Milwaukee Road hoped, sell the *Hiawathas* more vigorously on through ticketings.

At Rondout, after the train had been wyed at the diamond crossing with the Elgin, Joliet & Eastern, there was a ceremony.

"I christen thee 'Super Dome,'" said Jane Kiley, daughter of Milwaukee Road president John, before anointing the mammoth car with commingled waters from nearby Lake Michigan and far-off Puget Sound. In keeping with the *Hiawatha* theme, Indian headdresses were given out aboard the train, and there were corsages in Milwaukee Road colors for the women. Though the huge group of potential *Hiawatha* promoters were split up into two groups for morning and afternoon excursions, everyone lunched together at the Fred Harvey lunchroom and cafeteria at Chicago's Union Station.

Start-up of Super Dome revenue service was set for January 1, 1953, though cars were actually fed into

In July 1966 at Chicago, it's a sea of Omaha orange and green, with no shortage of domes, as the westbound *Empire Builder* makes its afternoon departure for Seattle. Behind it, equipment from the previously arrived eastbound *Builder* is pulled from Union Station by a Burlington switcher. (Peter Tilp)

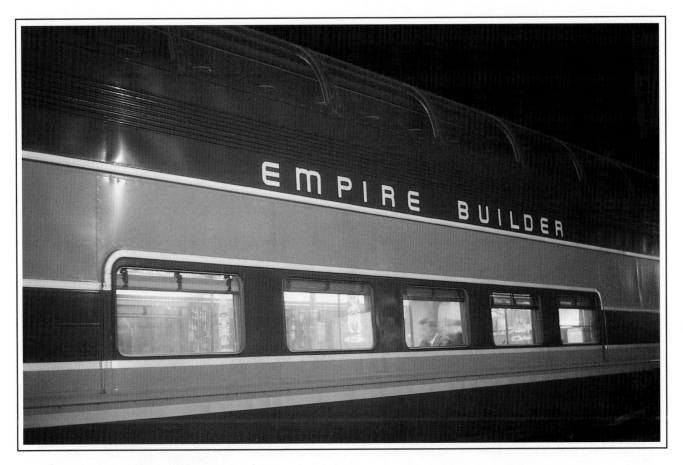

With dome lights properly darkened for visibility, the lounge area of the westbound *Empire Builder's* Great Dome shines a cozy welcome at Fargo, North Dakota. (Bob Johnston)

the *Olympian Hiawatha* consists beginning some ten days in advance of that date. For five years following, an operational status quo prevailed, with a single Super Dome running as planned in each *Olympian, Morning,* and *Afternoon Hiawatha* consist. Then in 1958 the *Olympian Hi* was combined east of Minneapolis with the *Morning/Afternoon Hiawathas,* freeing two Super Domes; in 1961 the train died entirely, freeing all six. The spare cars turned up for a time in the Union Pacific *Challenger* and "City" trains (which the Milwaukee Road had handled between Chicago and Council Bluffs, Nebraska, since 1955) and in some short hauls, notably Chicago–Madison, Wisconsin. By 1957, the domes — and virtually all Milwaukee Road passenger stock — wore the UP's yellow-and-gray "Streamliner" colors, reflecting the road's new Overland Route partnership.

Then, in 1964, the six surplus Super Domes went to Canadian National for operation through the Rockies in *Super Continental* and *Panorama* consists between Winnipeg or Edmonton and Vancouver. CN named them after rivers: Jasper, Athabaska, Yellowhead, Fraser, Qu'Apelle, and Columbia.

The next full-length domes to appear were 14 cars built by Budd for the Santa Fe and delivered in 1954. Constructed of stainless steel, they weighed just 96 tons, as compared to 112 tons for Pullman-Standard's Milwaukee Road Super Domes. Called "Big Domes" on Santa Fe, the fleet included eight cars for the Chicago–Los Angeles *El Capitan* and the *Chicagoan/Kansas Cityan,* and six for the soon-to-be-inaugurated *San Francisco Chief* from Chicago. Two years later, when the *El Cap* went to double-deck "Hi-Level" equipment, its Big Domes would go to the Chicago–Los Angeles *Chief.*

Santa Fe's two styles of Big Dome varied little, sharing an upper-level configuration of 57 coach seats and an 18-seat lounge, which lent a visual variety to the vast penthouse space that the Milwaukee domes lacked. The tables in this cocktail area were notable.

"Imbedded in the translucent Lucite tops are feathery sprays of Australian seaweed," according to *Railway Age.* "At night, when the overhead lights are turned off for passengers to observe the scenery from the coach seats forward, a light under the fixed ash

77

GREAT DOMES ON THE GREAT NORTHERN

The Great Northern Railway is an engineering masterpiece blessed by some of the most wonderful scenery in America.

Its Empire Builder glides past towering Rocky Mountains in Glacier National Park . . . along jade rivers and white-capped Puget Sound . . . through the forested Cascades . . . on its super-scenic trail between Chicago, St. Paul-Minneapolis, Spokane, Seattle and Portland.

Here are sights to thrill you, watching through the enormous curved windows of the new stainless steel dome cars, built by Budd, which now distinguish the Great Northern's Empire Builder.

The Great Northern, in company with many other railroads, has made every imaginative provision to make your trip by train the most restful, the most stimulating way to travel . . . the safest and most certain way to reach your destination . . . sprinkled all over with enjoyment.

To provide this feast of travel perfection, railroads call on Budd.

Philadelphia   Detroit   Gary

The Budd Company built all the *Empire Builder's* Great Domes — short and full-length — and advertised them with a Leslie Ragan painting. (Author's Collection)

tray above each table support glows through the lucite to produce a sunray effect."

The first series of Santa Fe Big Domes delivered — Nos. 506–513, for *El Cap* and the *Chicagoan/Kansas Cityan* — had a 28-seat bar-lounge downstairs and a room for a courier-nurse. Numbers 550–555, for the *San Francisco Chief,* had a much smaller lounge on the lower level, which left room for a crew dormitory sleeping 12.

Great Northern's five full-length domes (plus one owned by partner Burlington), delivered by Budd in 1955 for service on the Chicago–Seattle/Portland *Empire Builder,* were virtually identical in interior configuration to Santa Fe's 506-series cars. The only difference: Six extra lower-level lounge seats replaced the courier-nurse's room. The GN-CB&Q cars were the only full-length domes to carry names when new: Glacier View, Ocean View, Mountain View, Lake View, Prairie View, and River View.

The lower-level lounge was decorated with the colorful and powerful art of the Haida, or North Pacific Coast, Indians. The cars were reserved for Pullman passengers.

Among Western railroads rushing to embrace the dome car to keep up with the competition, Southern Pacific remained ambivalent. The party line was that clearances through the railroad's many tunnels and snowsheds were inadequate for full-size domes. This doctrine, which caused the dome areas aboard the *California Zephyr* to be emptied on occasions when that train detoured over SP's Donner Pass, was enforced into the Amtrak era, though the eventual routine operation of double-deck Superliners over these lines casts some retrospective doubt on the policy.

But Espee wasn't to be domeless. In July 1954, from the road's own Sacramento Shops rolled No. 3600, a handsome three-quarter-length dome constructed on the stripped-down frame of a round-end lightweight observation-parlor built in 1937. To satisfy the perceived clearance problem, the dome extended just 20 inches above the roof line — fully eight inches lower than Budd short domes — which virtually eliminated forward visibility. Design drawings were created by engineers and draftsmen in the motive-power office.

At one end of the car, on the main level, there was a small cocktail lounge seating 16. Since the dome extended over it, and since the lounge's side windows were five feet wide, this was an impressive space, with an 11-foot-high ceiling of glass. From this room passengers climbed stairs to the dome area proper — "Stairway to the Stars" was Espee's name for these cars — where low-backed seats for 44 passengers

were attractively arranged in a variety of groupings. At the rear end were 28 coach-like seats, angled slightly outward for good viewing. Forward was a 20-seat cocktail lounge, with wood-trimmed sofas grouped around six cocktail tables. Total seating capacity for the car was 64.

The car's interior furnishings were "characterized by simplicity," according to Claude E. Peterson, vice-president for system passenger service, and were "in the manner of the best Pacific Coast contemporary design." The work of Maurice Sands, a San Francisco designer, the space featured a color palette of greens for upholstery and carpeting, accented by the browns of teak and rattan.

The design compromise forced on the car by its low profile was insufficient room under the dome area for anything but machinery — no buffet lounge, no rest rooms, not even a passageway, so passengers had to climb up, then back down, to move through the train. Another factor here, most likely, was the impracticality of modifying the existing underframe to dip beneath the dome — the same problem Burlington had faced in converting Silver Dome and Silver Castle.

Resplendent in stylish orange and red *Daylight* dress, the car made its first run, between Sacramento and Oakland, on July 24. On board were representatives of all the crafts engaged in its conversion: mechanics, inside finishers, painters, the schedule foreman and truck foreman, lead workmen, sheet-metal men, air conditioners, and others, along with their wives. ("Like riding on a cloud" was mechanic C. Oschner's comment.) Railroad officials rode later that day. On July 26 the car entered revenue service in the consist of the St. Louis–San Francisco *San Francisco Overland.*

This prototype was well received when tested on the *Overland* and various other "name" trains, so half-a-dozen sisters were constructed in Sacramento, appearing in March through May of 1955, in time to enter service for the summer season. Basically similar to 3600, Nos. 3601 through 3606 were all slightly longer — 85 feet compared to 81 feet 2 inches — and carried more glass on both the upper and lower levels. Nos. 3601–3604 had 58 seats on the upper level and 20 on the lower; Nos. 3605–3606 had 54 and 20. These cars were very stylish indeed, with the bright openness of the main-floor cocktail room and the attractive groupings of sofas and tables at one end of the dome. From a practical point of view, however, the seating capacity totals of between 64 and 78 didn't stack up very well when compared, for instance, to the 96 seats in Milwaukee's Super Domes or 109 in GN's full-length Great Domes.

Initially domes 3600 and 3604 were assigned to the San Francisco–Los Angeles *San Joaquin Daylight*, 3605 and 3606 to the San Francisco–Portland *Shasta Daylight*, and 3601–3603 to the *San Francisco Overland* between Ogden and San Francisco. Cars 3601–3603 were dressed in gray and yellow Overland Route livery, while the other four cars wore *Daylight* red and orange.

For their first year and a half in service, the *San Joaquin's* domes experienced a rare meeting of the traditional and the modern as steam-locomotive exhaust swirled past their expansive glass. With GS-class daylight 4-8-4s routinely holding down the Oakland–Bakersfield segment of the run until September 1956, the *San Joaquin Daylight* was perhaps the only dome train to be hauled by steam on a regular basis. (In 1948 the *Exposition Flyer* routinely carried domes destined for the *CZ*, and at that time steam was still pinch-hitting for diesels frequently on that train, both on the Western Pacific and on the Rio Grande. And when the ex-*Chessie* domes entered *Royal Gorge* service in 1949, they too no doubt had their glass dusted now and then with cinders from Rio Grande steam.)

Southern Pacific's dome cars continued in their initial assignments for a number of years, though in time the erosion of passenger amenities (which occurred early and virulently on SP) led to some reassignments. The beginning of the end for the lovely *Shasta Daylight* with its stunning scenery through the Cascades came in 1959, when the train was reduced in frequency to triweekly in the off-season. In 1964 it became a summer-only service, then made its last run two years later. By then the *San Joaquin Daylight* was no longer featuring domes on a regular basis.

The SP domes had staying power on the Overland Route; when the *San Francisco Overland* was combined in the early sixties with the *City of San Francisco*, the latter train finally became a domeliner. And in the late sixties the *Coast Daylight* also sported domes in summer, the ones that once ran on its *Shasta* and *San Joaquin* brethren. Appearance as well as assignment changed, when beginning in 1959 the cars molted *Daylight* and Overland dress for the simplified silver scheme with red-orange numberboard that the SP passenger fleet wore at the end. Later the fluting below the windows was removed.

In spite of the superlatives accorded the full-length domes and Espee's home-builds, they all had their limitations. The most serious was the lack of forward visibility, the very characteristic of the Electro-Motive F-unit cab that led the creative Mr. Osborn to think up the dome car. High bulkheads, low seats, and the very length of the cars made it difficult to see either coming or going. Furthermore, the enormous glass area made them difficult to cool, particularly when air-conditioning units began to age. And they tended to be rough riders.

Nevertheless the cars did retain their attraction and cachet. As evidence of this, in late 1971 and early 1972 — immediately post-Amtrak — the Auto-Train Corporation grabbed 13 of Santa Fe's Big Domes. (The fourteenth remains in Santa Fe special train service today.) Amtrak took the six *Empire Builder* cars, five of the SP cars, plus the four Milwaukee Super Domes not sold to CN.

Years later, in 1985, Amtrak, in its limited program to modify a few dome cars to head-end power for continuing service, rebuilt three ex-GN full-length domes for its own *Auto Train* to Florida. And in 1991 *Auto Train* added full-length dome diners for sleeping-car passengers — former Milwaukee Road/Canadian National Super Domes acquired from Princess Tours and reconfigured. Ex-Santa Fe/Auto-Train Big Domes still run in Alaska today.

Whatever their shortcomings, the vast, glassed vehicles will get your attention, even in the 1990s.

THE *HIAWATHAS:* SPEED AND SCENERY

The saga of the Super Dome-carrying *Hiawathas* is a simple one — simple but elegant.

At first, back at its inaugural in 1935, the name was just *Hiawatha*, singular, as it was *Zephyr* and *Eagle*. And as in those cases, proliferation eventually demanded adjectival differentiation.

The *Hiawatha* entered service on the Chicago–St. Paul–Minneapolis run on May 29, 1935, destined for a career in fierce competition with Burlington's *Twin Zephyrs* and Chicago & North Western's *400s*. In January of 1939 the *Morning Hiawatha* (on the same route) was born, and the original train became the *Afternoon Hiawatha*. Eventually there would be a *North Woods Hiawatha*, a *Midwest Hiawatha*, a *Chippewa Hiawatha*.

The early *Hiawathas* were wonderfully idiosyncratic homemade affairs. Powered by dramatically stream-styled steam locomotives — Atlantics and Hudsons, most notably — and stocked with a flood of stylish cars built at the railroad's Milwaukee Shops, these trains were memorable indeed.

Then in 1947 came the Chicago–Seattle/Tacoma *Olympian Hiawatha* — truly a train fit for the gods. This train ushered in a new era for Milwaukee Road, one that sprang largely from the drawing boards of Brooks Stevens, a local industrial designer whose work included the "Skytop" observation cars, worthy

Here Southern Pacific's prototype dome, No. 3600, shows off handsome *Daylight* colors. This was the only car built with the shorter, ten-bay dome. (Southern Pacific: *Trains* Magazine Collection)

No. 3601, the first of the "production run" of six additional rebuilds, was among the trio dressed in Union Pacific colors for service on the *San Francisco Overland*. These six cars were longer than prototype 3600 and had two additional dome bays. (Peter Tilp Collection)

successors to the Beaver Tails that had carried the markers on earlier trains. The Skytops, whose convex round end was 90 percent glass, could easily be considered honorary dome cars.

The *Olympian Hi* was inaugurated on June 29, 1947, replacing the heavyweight *Olympian* that had long been the Milwaukee Road's prestige transcontinental service. The train ran with heavyweight Pullman and open-platform observation cars through the end of 1948, until Pullman-Standard could deliver Lake-series sleepers and Creek-series Skytops to replace them.

By this time the Twin Cities *Hiawathas* — *Morning* and *Afternoon* — already had their own "honorary dome cars": Rapids-series Skytop parlors. About four years later, at the end of 1952, when the real things arrived — the ten Pullman-Standard Super Domes — the Twin Cities *Hiawathas* became even better. And the *Olympian Hiawatha* became a dream train.

It had exotic motive power: Bipolars and Little Joes under wire, plus rare Fairbanks Morse "Erie-Builts." It had a stunningly scenic route through the mountains of Montana, Idaho, and Washington, with canyons, rivers, bridges, and tunnels beyond counting. It had sleepers, a diner, a Skytop Lounge, and now a Super Dome.

Unhappily, what it didn't have before too long was patronage. The remoteness of the route, one of the train's greatest charms, became a liability. In 1958 the *Olympian Hi* was combined with the *Morning* and *Afternoon Hiawathas* east of the Twin Cities, and eventually one of the two domes was deleted from the consolidated consist. In March 1959 the Skytop became seasonal. In May of 1961 the *Olympian Hiawatha*, dream train, died, among the first major casualties of a wrenching decade of discontinuances for the American passenger train.

The Twin Cities–Chicago *Hiawathas* fared much better, making it through most of that decade intact, Skytops and Super Domes and all. Finally, though, in January of 1970, the *Afternoon Hiawatha* was discontinued, leaving just its *Morning* twin to play out the string. That train ran right up to Amtrak, domed to the end.

THE *EMPIRE BUILDER:* THE MOST SEATS UNDER GLASS

No railroad mogul of the nineteenth century has a more lasting and fitting memorial than Great Northern's James J. Hill, the "Empire Builder," whose famous moniker survives even today in Amtrak's timetable.

Ever since its inauguration on June 10, 1929, the Chicago–Seattle/Portland *Empire Builder* has been a classy service, as was its direct predecessor, the *Oriental Limited.* The 1929 train, built largely by the Pullman Company, was both stylish and innovative. Instead of the traditional brass-railed observation platform, for instance, the solarium observation-lounge offered a sun room, furnished in wicker and enclosed against the elements, cinders, and road dust. Poking up on the roof of the car's hind end was a searchlight to illuminate the passing scenery — an idea resurrected 20 years later by the B&O with the floodlights on its dome cars.

The *Empire Builder* entered the streamline era on April 23, 1947, when five consists of gleaming orange and green Pullman-Standard cars entered service. With this inaugural GN stole the march on the competition; the *North Coast Limited's* lightweight cars would be trickled into the consist piecemeal in 1947 and 1948, with no formalities, and the streamlined *Olympian Hiawatha* would hit the rails four months after the streamlined *Builder.*

Just four years later, in time for the 1951 summer season, an all-new "Mid-Century *Empire Builder*" replaced these still nearly pristine consists, which in turn became the *Western Star,* a new secondary streamliner on the Builder's Chicago–Seattle/Portland route. This new rolling stock, delivered in roughly equal proportion by Pullman-Standard and American Car & Foundry at a cost of $12 million, included coaches, lunch-counter lounge, sleepers, diner, and buffet lounge-observation. Then four years later came the domes.

"Beginning May 29th!" trumpeted ads run in the spring of 1955, "Great Domes on the Great Northern's *Empire Builder!*" In addition to ballyhooing the "fastest streamliner from Chicago to Seattle" (thanks to a one-hour schedule cut made the day the domes would be introduced), the copy also promised the "newest and most modern dome cars to Pacific Northwest cities," which, in fact, were already served by a pair of domeliners from the Midwest: the *North Coast Limited* and the *Olympian Hi.* (Domes were about to appear from the south in the San Francisco–Portland *Shasta Daylight,* and Portland–Seattle pool service had featured UP's ex-*Train of Tomorrow* domes since 1950.)

"More Great Domes are on the way," the ad went on, "including luxurious full-length dome cars." (GN publicity routinely and specifically referred to all *Empire Builder* domes — including the short-dome coaches — as "Great Domes," presumably after the

"Great" in "Great Northern," rather than as an allusion to their size. However, the term has come to be applied only to the full-length cars.)

In each consist there would be three Budd short domes for coach passengers and one full-length dome for Pullman passengers — 147 dome seats in toto, the most ever. All the nonrevenue space in the View-series full-length domes — 75 seats upstairs, plus 34 in the lower-level lounge — made the Mountain-series observations (all-lounge except for two roomettes, used for passenger representative and Pullman conductor) an embarrassment of riches. Thus they were swapped with the *Western Star's* ex-*Builder* River-series observations, which were rebuilt as four-double-bedroom one-compartment six-roomette cars with very small lounge sections (sans buffet) at the observation end.

Renamed in the Coulee series, these cars were before long relegated to operation during the peak summer season only. After they left the consist in the fall of 1967 they never returned. Without observation car but still rich in domes, by 1968 wearing Great Northern's new Big Sky Blue scheme (which might have looked better had it not replaced the knockout orange-and-green livery) and finally, beginning in 1970, Burlington Northern's Cascade green and white, the *Builder* ran up to and into the Amtrak era.

6

American Car & Foundry's
"Daily Domeliners" for Union Pacific

Beginning with the little *City of Salina* of 1934, Union Pacific's yellow Streamliners were some of the best and brightest trains ever to burnish rail. Nevertheless, UP was relatively late among the Western transcontinentals in making the commitment to dome cars, the *ne plus ultra* of the private passenger train's final years. But once in the race, UP made a fine showing indeed.

Just before Christmas in 1952, Union Pacific placed an order for 70 passenger cars from American Car & Foundry, and in early 1953 the railroad announced that 15 of these cars would be domes: five

chair cars, five diners, and five observation-lounges. By the time of UP's order, CB&Q, D&RGW, WP, Mopac, B&O, Santa Fe, and Wabash were all running domes, and Milwaukee Road had Super Domes on the property and poised to enter service.

Of course, UP itself by then was already a dome operator in a small way, having purchased the *Train of Tomorrow* from GM in 1950. The four cars had been placed in Seattle–Portland pool-train service (NP and GN were the other partners), perhaps for lack of a better assignment, since singleton cars were not of much use to the multiconsist transcontinentals. The main

By August 1957, when No. 105, the *City of Portland*, was caught sweeping west through Archer, Wyoming, at 60 miles an hour, dome lounge No. 9004 had been modified for midtrain operation. Immediately ahead of it is the dome diner, and two cars farther forward the dome coach. (Richard Kindig)

84

This very rare photo of the *Challenger* leaving Chicago's Chicago & North Western Terminal in April 1955 (UP trains switched to the Milwaukee Road and Union Station at the end of October) is proof that the *Challenger* did indeed carry, if only for a short time, the dome observations originally intended for it. (Larry Mack)

significance of this acquisition may well be that diner Sky View inspired UP to make dome diners its unique hallmark. And UP assumed for all its dome cars the name "Astra-Domes," coined for the *Train of Tomorrow*.

By the time of delivery, UP's dome order with ACF had burgeoned from 15 to 35 cars — 10 diners, 10 chair cars, and 15 observation-lounges — which arrived from ACF's St. Charles Plant in Missouri from December 1954 through May 1955. These were American Car & Foundry's first, last, and only dome cars — handsome, with fine visibility, and unique in that their domes were fabricated in one-piece sections of curved glass, while all short domes from Pullman-Standard and Budd used two sections to form the full curve.

The UP's dome cars were unusual in another way: They were the only domes to make significant use of aluminum in their construction. While the underframe was a low-alloy high-tensile riveted and welded steel assembly, the superstructure (except the dome frame and the car ends) was fabricated almost entirely of an aluminum alloy. Specifically, side sheathing, side plates, belt rail, and side posts (except those over the jacking pads) were aluminum.

While this aluminum construction was unique among dome cars, it was typical for UP streamliners — and had been right from the very beginning. The *City of Salina* — the original *Streamliner*, and also arguably the first "small-ess" streamliner to run on any railroad — was essentially all-aluminum; only the bolsters were steel. The years 1934–1941 saw the construction of nine more all-aluminum, articulated "Cities" train-sets, plus 50 aluminum cars for the prewar *Challenger*: nonarticulated coaches and twin-unit diners. (*Challenger* partners Chicago & North Western and Southern Pacific rostered 33 similar coaches as their contribution to the train's equipment pool.)

The subsequent evolution to 85-foot cars saw steel underframes replace aluminum, though aluminum was still used for body and roof. Retaining aluminum for the superstructure allowed the steel parts to be heavier and stronger without excessive total weight. Not

85

Aboard the *City of Los Angeles* in June 1970, the tables in the main level of the diner are laid with snowy linens and fresh flowers. (Bob Schmidt)

only that, the aluminum side and roof sheets could be much thicker — and thus more resistant to denting and collision damage — than if they were steel. And even with these increases in gauge for added strength, aluminum yielded a weight saving of 20,000 pounds per car, which translated to one or two extra cars in a consist on stiff grades through the mountains.

UP initially had some concerns about the dome cars' stability, but a series of "lean tests" showed a dome coach to evidence less static inward lean and less dynamic outward lean than the 1941 ACF lightweight sleeper used as the control in this experiment. The domes rode on General Steel Castings trucks with outside swing hangers, and this equipment was clearly up to the task.

The Chicago–Los Angeles *City of Los Angeles* initially received a dome diner and dome lounge-observation, while a dome chair car and, briefly, a dome lounge-observation went to the all-coach *Challenger* on that same route. The Chicago–Portland *City of Portland* carried a dome chair car, dome diner, and dome lounge-observation, making it the most dome-heavy UP train until the *Challenger* and *City of Los Angeles* were combined and equaled it. The St. Louis–Los Angeles *City of St.*

Louis received a dome lounge-observation after these cars made a cameo appearance on the *Challenger.* Wherever they ran, all 15 of the observations soon were modified for midtrain operation next to the diner.

The dome coaches and observations were delivered first, through the early months of 1955. The coaches had 36 seats on the main level, compared to 46 aboard the *CZ, North Coast Limited, Empire Builder,* and *Colorado Eagle,* which featured the lowest density of all the Budd-built dome coaches. (Budd's short-haul dome coaches carried as many as 54 main-level, revenue seats.) In addition to being spacious, the UP's coaches were unusually opulent in decor, with curtains, carpeting, and fully upholstered seats, including the arms. The men's and women's lounges were under the dome, also standard Budd practice.

In the long, trailing section, UP's blunt-end observations (soon to be midtrain lounges) had a comfortable lounge seating 21 in moveable chairs, settees, and sofas of various styles. Seats could be faced inward for conversation or outward for viewing. Drapes, attractively patterned carpet, and overstuffed yet stylishly modern chairs with curved backs gave the lounge the feeling of a well-turned-out middle-class living room.

Though they looked much like UP's other domes from the outside, the diners were special. The seats in the dome were choice. (Union Pacific Railroad)

At the front, short end of the car was a card room containing a round table ringed with six chairs. Under the dome was a nine-seat cocktail lounge and service bar. (This arrangement was similar to that typically found in Budd dome lounges, though these ACF cars differed in having full-sized windows in the under-dome room.) The back-bar mural depicted the Golden Spike ceremony at Promontory. The dome area of the chair cars and observation-lounges had divan-type seats, angled slightly toward the windows, accommodating 24 — the short-dome standard.

The ten dome diners, delivered beginning May 1955, were the gems of the fleet, with a lovely carpeted and curtained elegance that was more suggestive of a fine restaurant than the typical railroad dining car. The main dining room seated 18 at round tables for two or four, a unique arrangement that gave the area a remarkably spacious feel. Linens were originally pink in this room.

The dome likewise offered seating for 18 fortunate passengers — in comfortable booths, also for two or four. Tables here originally had golden-color cloths.

"The dome section," wrote Harry I. Norris, manager of UP's Dining Car and Hotel Department, in an article in *Railway Age*, "will allow travelers to have their meals without missing a minute of sightseeing. What we hope to provide is the exhilaration of dining under the open sky while the landscape races past."

Under the dome was the third dining area, a small "reserve" dining room, with two tables for five passengers each. Here green linens set off the gilded gleam of vermeil silverware. On the *City of Portland* cars, a pattern of roses in red silk-screen print (for Portland, "City of Roses") covered the white Formica walls, and a Columbia hybrid tea rose was etched into the glass partition to the passageway. Aboard the *City of Los Angeles*, the reserve dining room's green-on-white walls had patterns incorporating images of a movie camera, the L. A. skyline, Grauman's Chinese Theater, and a Hollywood movie premiere.

The three dining spaces together yielded a total of 46 seats; considering the car's spacious feel, this capacity stacks up well in comparison to the standard 48-seat diner, crowded with rectangular wall-supported tables, or the more comfortable (and relatively rare) 36-place version of the same, with 2-and-1 seating across.

Like all short domes, UP's were asymmetrical. The smaller end of the dome diners contained the main kitchen, while an adjacent pantry shared under-dome space with the reserve dining room, servicing it and the main dining room. The dome area had a small pantry as well, separated from the tables by a low glass partition. Food reached the dome by pneumatically operated dumb waiter from the main pantry, though the dome pantry had its own refrigerator, ice well, toasters, coffee urns, and sink.

Those precious dome seats — the "roof garden," as UP had it — were the place to be, no doubt, since their occupants were privileged to enjoy the twin pleasures of a tasty meal and a spectacular vista. Plates of Nebraska corn-fed beef, Columbia River salmon, or Utah mountain trout were set (later in the cars' careers) on pink linens. Outside, surrounding the passenger at table, one of the West's many scenic moods — sunset or snowstorm, sagebrush or mountain — provided the ultimate sense of well-being that no stationary restaurant could touch.

"While enjoying your selection of superb, freshly prepared foods," bragged UP, "you can feast your eyes on magnificent panoramic views stretching to the far horizon." The brochure copywriter concluded: "You'll find it to be a bright page in your book of memories." And one that, for the railroad, didn't come cheap. Not surprisingly, these Astra-Dome diners were expensive, costing about $300,000 each to build, and an additional $23,000 each to equip — a considerable amount of money at the time. Silverware alone — UP's own pattern, made by International Silver Company, cost more than $65,000 for the ten cars. Table linens cost $100,000, china and glassware $8,000, and crew uniforms (for 250 employees all told) $44,000.

In his *Railway Age* article, Norris put this expense in another context. "Last year," he wrote, "American railroads lost $35 million on dining car operations." So why spend all this money on dome diners?

"We consider these new diners a sound investment," he continued, echoing what was for decades the industry party line, "an investment in good will." Still, he pointed out, "the minute these dining cars are put in service, we'll start losing money on them. The more meals we serve, the more money we'll lose."

This was just one aspect of Union Pacific's commitment to excellent passenger service, maintained long after a like attitude was jettisoned by most other railroads. So it's not surprising that to UP (along with *City of St. Louis* partner Wabash) fell the distinction of

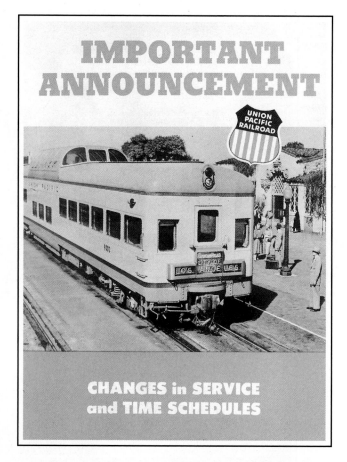

This October 1955 flyer announcing the winter consists of trains west from Chicago lists the *City of Portland* as carrying a dome dining car, observation-lounge, and coach; the *City of Los Angeles* a dome dining car and observation-lounge; and the *Challenger* a dome coach. It also announces the October 30 shift to the Milwaukee Road and Union Station. (Author's Collection)

taking delivery on what proved to be the last traditional domes ever built. In November and December 1958 UP 7011–7015 and Wabash 203 arrived from Pullman-Standard to supplement the ACF dome lounge-observations and make the *City of St. Louis* a two-dome train. These half-dozen cars, the only curved-glass short domes ever constructed by P-S (they followed ACF's specifications), brought that builder's dome total to 34. But with just the single UP order for 35 cars, ACF edged out Pullman-Standard's seven-railroad fleet.

Espee built seven on its own, and Burlington two. Budd achieved an overwhelming majority with 158 cars delivered. All these add up to 236 dome cars — the all-time total.

ASTRA-DOMES: THE CROWNING GLORY FOR THE GREAT "CITIES" FLEET

The Union Pacific's Streamliner history began in 1934 with the barnstorming three-car M-10000, the

On February 5, 1957, the eastbound *City of St. Louis* — with a dome observation-lounge that briefly served the *Challenger* — meets a freight extra at Summit, California. (Chard Walker)

Pullman-built, distillate-powered, articulated trainset that entered service on January 31, 1935, as the Kansas City–Topeka–Salina *City of Salina*. That history ended in the last years before Amtrak with the seemingly endless combined consist dubbed the "City of Everywhere," sometimes run in two sections and aggregating as many as 36 cars.

In between came a long yellow-and-gray line of "City" Streamliners: *City of Portland* (1935), *City of Los Angeles*, *City of San Francisco*, and *City of Denver* (all 1936), and — a late arrival and for many years something of a "poor relation" to the others — *City of St. Louis* (1946). A steady influx of new equipment — at first articulated cars, powered by unique and striking EMC diesels, later more standardized models of both cars and locomotives — increased the frequencies of all the trains to daily and later upgraded and modernized them.

The "Cities" streamliners were already among the premier passenger fleets when domes were added to the consists of some of them in 1955 as the tail end of a major postwar upgrade. Beginning in 1949 and continuing through the early fifties, a huge fleet of new cars arrived: RPOs, baggage cars, coaches, lounges, diners, sleepers. They came from all three major builders — Budd, ACF, and P-S — since the urgent need for cars broke down the UP's previously pure predilection for Pullman-Standard.

Then in late 1954 and early 1955 UP took delivery of yet another 59-car order from ACF, the one containing the Astra-Domes that made the *City of*

Portland, the *City of Los Angeles* (along with the *Challenger*, on the same route), and the *City of St. Louis* Domeliners.

The *City of Denver* was the next of the UP Streamliners to metamorphose into a Domeliner, and it did so in January 1958 with a pair of Super Domes owned by the Milwaukee Road, which on October 30, 1955, had succeeded Chicago & North Western as UP's Midwest partner, forwarding the Overland Route fleet east from Omaha to Chicago. These domes had become available when Milwaukee Road's Chicago–Seattle *Olympian Hiawatha* had begun running combined between Chicago and Minneapolis with the *Afternoon Hiawatha* (westbound) and the *Morning Hiawatha* (eastbound) in 1957. At first the combined trains had carried both domes, but by the end of the year one was dropped — and, wearing UP yellow dress, moved to the *City of Denver*.

This arrangement lasted just until January of 1959, when the *City of Portland* and *City of Denver* were consolidated, a compromise that lengthened the Portland train's run, costing it the competitive edge in timing over Great Northern's *Empire Builder*. Since the combined consist inherited the *City of Portland's* three ACF domes, the Super Domes were redundant and thus withdrawn.

The *City of San Francisco*, Nos. 101–102, was the last UP Streamliner to become a domeliner, and it did so largely by default, in September 1960, when it was combined with the *City of Los Angeles*. (Southern Pacific did also assign one of its low-profile domes to its

Although Ronald Reagan the actor enthusiastically pitched the Domeliners for UP, he lost his enthusiasm for train travel as a President hostile to Amtrak. (Author's Collection)

The *City of Los Angeles* was a spiffy train right through summer 1970, the last of the pre-Amtrak era. Here lounge No. 9011 and diner No. 8004 are carried east through Victorville, California. (Bob Schmidt)

portion of the run, Ogden–Oakland, so it wasn't entirely a case of addition by subtraction.)

These train consolidations were part of the contraction of services that, ironically, characterized the entire dome era on the UP. In the ten years beginning in 1952, passenger revenues shrank progressively every single year, dropping from $39.9 million to $27.5 million annually in the course of the ten-year period. Even as UP was ordering and introducing its glamorous fleet of dome cars, it was simultaneously feeling sharp declines in the passenger market.

This led to seasonal consolidations of the *City of Los Angeles* and *Challenger*, both Chicago–Los Angeles trains, as early as 1956, and the later *City of Portland-City of Denver* and *City of San Francisco-City of Los Angeles* combinations. As the sixties wore on, even more trains were melded together into the monumental consists known not entirely affectionately as the "City of Everywhere." *The City of St. Louis* was combined west of Ogden in 1967, and west of Cheyenne in 1968.

Another contraction in dome-car mileage came in 1969 when Norfolk & Western, successor through merger to Wabash in *City of St. Louis* partnership with UP, discontinued its portion of the train's run, the St. Louis–Kansas City leg. UP renamed its truncated train the *City of Kansas City,* a name that had just become available the previous year when N&W's St. Louis–Kansas City streamliner of that name, inaugurated by Wabash back in 1947, was discontinued.

Finally, after the 1969 season, the *City of Portland* was folded into the mix east of Green River, so that No. 103 leaving Chicago comprised the *City of Los Angeles* (and *Challenger*), *City of San Francisco*, *City of Portland,* and *City of Denver*, with *City of Kansas City* cars to be added at Cheyenne.

The dome diners were missing from this mélange in the final months, but a dome lounge — between Chicago and Los Angeles — and dome coaches — one each Chicago–Portland and Chicago–Los Angeles — remained to the end.

91

7

Hand-Me-Down Domes
New Lives for Old Cars

From 1958, when the last new domes ever built were delivered by Pullman-Standard for service on the *City of St. Louis,* until 1971, when Amtrak was formed and bought (eventually) 105 domes from the railroads, little change occurred in existing dome-car fleets. True, plenty of domes were pulled out of service in the last year or so prior to Amtrak — last-ditch attempts to moderate losses as the private railroads waited for the quasi-governmental savior to take passenger trains off their hands. But original dome operators Burlington, Rio Grande, Northern Pacific, Great Northern, Spokane, Portland & Seattle, Union Pacific, Southern Pacific, Santa Fe, Milwaukee Road, Baltimore & Ohio, and Wabash (by then part of Norfolk & Western) all fielded domes into the final days.

Though the vast majority of domes remained with their original owners for their entire pre-Amtrak careers, there were exceptions — and some movement right at the beginning. Probably the most well-traveled domes of all were the six originally built for the never-to-be streamliner *Chessie.* These cars were gone from Chesapeake & Ohio almost before they arrived from Budd. (In fact, many of the cars in C&O's big postwar order were actually directed to other roads before ever being delivered to their initial purchaser.)

The C&O's dome sleepers never entered regular C&O service. The first to go, however, were the coach-observation-lounges, sold to the Denver & Rio Grande Western in September 1949 after a brief stint in Michigan carrying the markers on the Detroit–Grand Rapids *Pere Marquette* streamliners. Rio Grande converted the cars for midtrain operation by boxing the round ends and adding diaphragms before placing

them in service on the Denver–Colorado Springs–Salt Lake City *Royal Gorge.* Rio Grande was already a dome operator, of course, hosting Vista-Domes on MoPac's *Colorado Eagle* between Pueblo, Colorado, and Denver since the summer of 1948. The *California Zephyr* had arrived in March 1949 (and its dome cars had run in the *Exposition Flyer* a full year earlier).

For the Rio Grande this trio of ex-C&O domes, which D&RGW renumbered 1248–1250, was just a small part of a much-needed infusion of new equipment, all directly or indirectly courtesy of Chesapeake & Ohio. The Budd-built domes were purchased outright from C&O. However, the Rio Grande acquired an additional 25 cars — Pullmans, coaches, diners, buffet-lounges, and head-end cars — by taking over "delivery positions" from C&O on equipment that Robert Young, his eyes bigger than his stomach, had over-ordered. These cars went directly from Pullman-Standard to D&RGW at prices that reflected the economies of scale of C&O's huge order, and without delivery delays.

With all this new equipment came a striking new paint scheme: stainless steel below, "Grande Gold" (a vivid orange, actually) above, adorned with four narrow black bands. Diesels were painted to match, and this became D&RGW's standard dress for both cars and cab-unit diesels.

The new equipment was ample to re-equip both the overnight Denver–Salt Lake *Prospector* on the direct Moffat Tunnel route (also taken by the *California Zephyr*) and the *Royal Gorge,* which served the same endpoints by making a deep detour south to Colorado Springs and Pueblo, Colorado, before angling northwest to traverse the Royal Gorge — the Grand Canyon of the Arkansas River — and cross the Continental Divide at 10,221-foot Tennessee Pass.

The *Royal Gorge*, Nos. 1 and 2, already had an illustrious history as a steam-powered heavyweight by the time it became a diesel domeliner. Its direct lineal ancestor was the *Scenic Limited*, which was renamed the *Royal Gorge* in 1946. This was a most appropriate handle, since that natural feature had always provided the train's most memorable moments — ten minutes, specifically, the length of time Nos. 1 and 2 traditionally paused at Hanging Bridge, deep in the Gorge, to let passengers disembark to gawk at the canyon wall soaring vertically above. (So precipitous are the walls of this chasm that, at its narrowest, no ledge could be cut for the tracks, so a bridge was hung to carry them over the Arkansas's turbulent flow.)

"Now," read the timetable copy for the streamliner, "the see-all Vista-Dome car adds thrilling perspective to make the *Royal Gorge* a brand new travel delight." And though the dome car's vertical sightlines somewhat diminished the need for the Hanging Bridge stop, the streamlined *Royal Gorge* always paused there for the prescribed ten minutes, just as its heavyweight predecessors had.

In addition to the domes, the streamlined *Royal Gorge* carried flat-top coaches, a heavyweight Pullman (ten sections, three double bedrooms, summer-only, painted in the new streamliner colors), and a grill-lounge, which gave way to a heavyweight diner-lounge in summer to meet the demands of greater patronage. On February 11, 1950 — not long after the arrival of the domes — Nos. 1 and 2 were combined between Grand Junction and Salt Lake with the *Prospector*, Nos. 7 and 8, making the latter a domeliner for part of its run. This arrangement, initiated to conserve motive power during a coal strike, worked so well that it was continued for the life of the trains. In the case of the *Royal Gorge*, it made a slow train even slower (23 hours Denver–Salt Lake, as opposed to less than 14 for the *California Zephyr*), but scenery was the train's *raison d'être* for long-distance passengers anyway.

In 1956, with the re-equipping of the Chicago–Denver *Denver Zephyr* (and inauguration of its Colorado Springs extension), another dome entered the *Royal Gorge* picture, as that train carried the *DZ's* through cars from Denver to Colorado Springs. At first these included the Chuck Wagon dome, and later a dome coach.

The status quo prevailed until December 1966, when the *Royal Gorge* was discontinued west of Salida, Colorado. Immediately after that, on January 1, 1967, the *Denver Zephyr's* Colorado Springs cars vanished. In

May the *Prospector* died, and in July what was left of the *Royal Gorge* did too. That left D&RGW with just the *CZ*, the steam-powered Silverton Train hauling tourists through the San Juan Mountains, and a once-obscure little plug run, the Denver–Craig, Colorado, *Yampa Valley Mail*, Nos. 9 and 10.

In the fall of 1966, a few months before the *Royal Gorge* was truncated at Salida, the dome-coach-lounges — the last of the through cars to be handed over to the *Prospector* at Grand Junction — had been transferred to the *Yampa Valley Mail*. This helped assure that the short, modest consist that served what had once been the main line of David Moffat's Denver & Salt Lake would emerge into the spotlight for its final days. On April 7, 1968, it too was discontinued.

But this still wasn't the end for the Rio Grande's domes. After nearly two decades of yeoman service on the Grande these cars were retired in 1970, then sold. Number 1249 went to Chapman S. Root in Daytona, Florida, where it was named Silver Holly and rebuilt with four bedrooms, a kitchen, and a plush lounge for use as a private car. Number 1250 was sold to Auto-Liner Corporation in 1970, acquiring the name Linoma. Initially leased to Amtrak, Linoma was sold to the carrier in 1974. After retirement in 1976 it went out to pasture at the Choo Choo Hilton in Chattanooga, where it remained until acquisition in 1994 for display by the Tennessee Valley Railroad, a Chattanooga rail museum.

Most interesting of all is No. 1249, which went to Butterworth Tours of Davenport, Iowa. Named Big Ben, the car received modifications that included the addition of tables in the dome and replacement of the coach seats in the forward section of the car with booths and lounge chairs. Under a special agreement, Butterworth offered first-class service on a regular basis aboard Big Ben in Rock Island's Chicago–Rock Island, Illinois, *Quad City Rocket* — really a long-distance commuter train — through much of the 1970s.

With Southern and Rio Grande, Rock Island declined to join Amtrak in 1971. (Each of the three major "separatists" had its own reasons; Rock Island's was that it lacked the cash to pay the entrance fee.) The result was that, under Butterworth auspices, this well-traveled dome had yet another successful career, until the *Quad City Rocket* (along with the *Peoria Rocket*) was discontinued on January 1, 1979. In December 1993 Frank Dowd, Jr., donated Big Ben to the Chesapeake & Ohio Historical Society, which hopes to restore the car to its as-built appearance.

The three dome sleepers intended for the *Chessie* also had respectably long careers with their first

On New Year's Eve of 1966, the *Yampa Valley Mails* meet at Radium, Colorado. The train had inherited the domes just a few months earlier; with the handsome PAs on the point, the *Yampa Valley Mail* suddenly became a short but intriguing train. (Steve Patterson: *Trains* Magazine Collection)

stepparents, in this case the Baltimore & Ohio. In December of 1950 two of the cars entered *Capitol Limited* service, with the third serving the *Shenandoah* on alternate days. These ex-Chessie domes remained on the *Cap* until October 1965, when the P-S domes, available since the *Columbian's* discontinuance in April 1964, became the *Capitol's* for the brief remainder of the train's career. (The third sleeper-dome had gone out of *Shenandoah* service in October 1963.)

This made all three of the ex-*Chessie* cars surplus on B&O, so from December 1965 to April 1966, still in Pullman lease, they ran on Atlantic Coast Line's seasonal New York–Miami *Florida Special*. (Rare among domes, these cars were sleepers and thus operated by Pullman.) In May of 1966 they went out of Pullman lease and, from then until May of 1968, were leased by B&O to Canadian National, where they ran sporadically (primarily in summer) in *Super Continental* and

Panorama service, between Vancouver and Edmonton, joining the six Super Domes CN had purchased from the Milwaukee Road two years earlier.

In June of 1968 the cars went back into Pullman lease and that fall ran Richmond–Miami in Seaboard Coast Line's *Silver Star*. (Atlantic Coast Line and Seaboard Air Line had merged the previous year.) In December the cars were shifted to the *Florida Special*, running there until the train's seasonal suspension in April. The domes had big shoes to fill as the *Special's* feature cars, which the previous year had been ex-*Broadway* observations Mountain View and Tower View and ex-*Crescent* Royal-series observations.

The sleeper domes operated south of Richmond only, reportedly because of clearance restrictions through the Capitol Hill Tunnel into Washington Union Station. This raises interesting questions, since the Washington–Cincinnati *Chessie,* the train for which the cars had been built some 20 years earlier, would have traversed that same tunnel had it ever operated as originally intended. The rumor persists that Robert Young had ordered the train before ever working out this significant detail, and that in fact the tunnel had been the ill-fated *Chessie's* first major embarrassment.

Counterarguments hold that, though there were soluble problems with platform clearance at Washington, the tunnel itself was not an issue. And without question there were other factors, both financial and competitive, that led to the *Chessie's* demise. With the passage of time, however, circumstantial evidence suggests that the inability of the much-touted domes to get through the Capitol Hill Tunnel may well have been the immediate reason for the train's premature abandonment.

On January 1, 1969, a long and illustrious tradition came to an end when Pullman ceased operation of sleeping cars; on August 1, they stopped maintaining them as well. At that point, by prearrangement, B&O sold Moonlight Dome, Starlight Dome, and Sunlight Dome to Hamburg Industries, an SCL subsidiary set up to maintain the line's passenger cars in lieu of Pullman. (When Hamburg Industries refurbished the dome cars, they inexplicably blanked out the top windows with a padded ceiling.) Then for two more winters the dome trio served the *Florida Special*.

Amtrak inherited the cars, using them initially on the Chicago–Miami *South Wind*. Later assignments included the Chicago–Oakland *San Francisco Zephyr*, where their lower-than-usual profiles eased Southern Pacific's fears about running domes through their tunnels and snowsheds. (Even so, SP insisted that the cars be re-equipped with outside swing-hanger trucks to prevent "excessive car rocking," feared to be a problem in tunnels.)

After C&O unloaded its *Chessie* cars in 1949–50, no domes changed hands until 1964. That year, the six Milwaukee Road Super Domes made surplus by the discontinuance of the *Olympian Hiawatha* were sold, along with the train's six Skytop sleeper-observations, to Canadian National to run through the Rockies on the *Super Continental* and *Panorama*, beating the leased B&O domes into this service by two years. CN called the ex-Hiawatha cars "Sceneramic Domes" (a name reminiscent of competitor CP's "Scenic Domes") and made considerable modifications on the upper level, with many rows of lock-step coach seating giving way to lounge groupings with banquettes and cocktail tables, and some swiveling parlor-style chairs. This gave the space a friendlier feel, though nothing could be done about the lack of forward visibility.

The Sceneramic Domes, along with the sleeper domes for the two years they were on the property, operated in ever-changing patterns on CN's west end — between Vancouver and Winnipeg, where the scenery was. Assignments changed in summer, when the Toronto and Montreal sections of the *Super Continental* ran as separate trains. At times only the *Panorama* was a domeliner, and at times only the *Super Continental*. Then the *Panorama* was discontinued, in January 1970, leaving the *Super Continental* as CN's lone dome operation. In any case, a Sceneramic Dome switched into the consist for some part of a trip was hardly competitive with the pair of Budd-built short domes fielded for every mile to both Toronto and Montreal by CP's *Canadian*.

The next significant second-hand dome acquisition was Illinois Central's purchase in June 1967 of six dome chair cars from Missouri Pacific and Texas & Pacific: the three 1948 Budd domes and three of Pullman-Standard's 1952 cars. In December they entered service on the Chicago–New Orleans *City of New Orleans*. This train would carry two of these dome coaches, while one (usually a Budd car) would be included in the *City of Miami*, an every-other-day Chicago–Florida service that was already a dome veteran, operating leased Northern Pacific dome sleepers during the winter seasons through much of the sixties.

The Illinois Central domes wore the road's smart chocolate-and-orange dress, but their attractiveness was severely compromised by steel plates that replaced the end windows in both Budd and Pullman-Standard domes — an unfortunate expedient even more bizarrely counterproductive than SCL's padded ceilings. The railroad pulled domes off its trains in February 1971, long after IC and virtually everybody else had given up on passenger trains. But at least briefly after their purchase, before the dispiriting service erosion of the final years had begun, those newly acquired domes added a final touch of class to the *City of New Orleans* and *City of Miami* — proud trains still carrying diners and round-end club lounge-observation cars.

Almost immediately on the heels of the Illinois Central acquisitions came more domes for the deep south, when Norfolk & Western first leased (in January 1968) and then sold (in December 1969) to Southern Railway subsidiary Central of Georgia the Pullman-Standard dome parlor built for *Blue Bird* service. Central of Georgia placed this dome on the *Nancy Hanks II*, a pocket streamliner that ran between Atlanta and Savannah and numbered a grill-lounge among its amenities. A single-consist service, the train covered the 290-mile route westbound in morning and eastbound in the afternoon.

Aboard the dome parlor, the under-dome lounge that had been the "Blue Bird Room" became the "Saddle and Stirrup Room," appropriate for a train named after a racehorse. In October 1970 this car was transferred to the parent road's *Southern Crescent* for use on the train's Atlanta–New Orleans leg. As a replacement on *Nancy Hanks II,* Central of Georgia purchased from N&W the 1958 Pullman-Standard dome coach that had been Wabash's contribution to the *City of St. Louis* pool.

After the discontinuance of the *Nancy Hanks II* at Amtrak's creation, Southern moved the dome coach to Nos. 3 and 4, a triweekly Asheville–Salisbury, North Carolina, remnant of the once-illustrious *Asheville Special,* a through train with Pullmans for New York and Washington. (While Southern stayed out of Amtrak and thus continued to operate its few remaining trains, subsidiary CofG joined and was allowed to drop its service.) Like *Nancy Hanks II,* Nos. 3 and 4 were also a single-consist train that ran out in the morning and back in late afternoon.

Its route was certainly worthy of a dome car, particularly the "Loops" area between Ridgecrest and Old Fort, at the Asheville end of the run, which featured an array of tunnels, fills, and curves adequate to turn any surveyor's hair gray. (The sprint across the Piedmont into Salisbury was admittedly less inspiring.) Patronage was as modest as the three-car train, however, and at the expiration of the waiting period mandated when Southern declined to join Amtrak, the railroad filed for discontinuance.

With permission granted by the North Carolina Utilities Commission, the Southern dropped Nos. 3 and 4 in July 1975. The following month, however, they commenced operation of the *Skyland Special,* a summer and fall weekends-only excursion train between Asheville and Old Fort. This three-and-a-half-hour round trip, which had been promised in the discontinuance application, covered the most scenic part of the line. Consist included an open car, as well as the dome. The FP7's that had powered 3 and 4 continued in *Skyland Special* service; for the 1976 season they appeared in the apple-green dress that had recently been introduced on the *Southern Crescent's* E-units.

For the first two seasons the train operated weekends from Memorial Day through Labor Day, plus three October weekends for the fall foliage. Patronage was disappointing, however, and in 1977 the *Special* operated only during foliage season. By this time the ex-*City of St. Louis* dome coach had been shifted to the *Southern Crescent,* with ex-*Blue Bird* dome parlor going to the *Skyland Special* in exchange. The *Special* was dropped; then, on February 1, 1979, the *Southern Crescent* became an Amtrak train, and the Southern Railway's brief but sweet domeliner era came to an end.

Once again dome coach No. 1613 — veteran of the *City of St. Louis, Nancy Hanks II, Skyland Special,* and *Southern Crescent* — was surplus. In 1979, therefore, Southern sold the car to the remote Quebec, North Shore & Labrador, making it among the most far-flung of all the domes. This isolated line, stretching 576 miles north from Sept Iles, on the Gulf of St. Lawrence, to Labrador City, hosts two passenger trains a week, as remote a venue as you're likely to find for a dome-car ride.

May 1, 1971: In retrospect, the birth of Amtrak now appears to have been the beginning of the end for significant dome operations in the United States. At its inception Amtrak did pick up well more than half the available domes, 105 out of roughly 180. (This makes it by far the largest operator of second-hand domes, enough to merit a separate chapter, which follows.) Because of a strong (and well-founded) prejudice for Budd's Shotwelded cars, where the fluted sides were structural, Amtrak turned up its nose at most P-S cars, domed and otherwise, where fluting was cosmetic, laid on top of Corten steel; moisture tended to gather in between, leading to corrosion.

A number of quality cars escaped in addition. Auto-Train, an independent company just gearing up to transport automobiles and their passengers from Lorton, Virginia, near Alexandria, to Sanford, Florida, grabbed 56 of the best domes, many of which Amtrak might well have acquired had it not been caught temporizing. Auto-Train's haul (in the initial purchase and a subsequent one in 1972) included Western Pacific's seven ex-*California Zephyr* Vista-Dome chair cars, all but one of Santa Fe's 14 Big Domes, and all but seven of Union Pacific's 40 domes — ten coaches, nine diners, and 14 lounges in all. (A considerable number of these would never be modified, painted in *Auto-Train* colors, or placed in service.)

The brainchild of Eugene Kerik Garfield, president and CEO (and former assistant to the then-Secretary of Transportation Alan Boyd), Auto-Train got off the blocks running when inaugurated in December 1971, about six months after Amtrak came into being. With its locomotives and cars painted red, white, and purple, *Auto-Train* was pointedly and radically new. Interior colors of crimson, purple, yellow, and red (not unlike the red-and-purple palette of Amtrak's early refurbishings) showed up on carpets, upholstery, and

After the *Yampa Valley Mail's* discontinuance in April of 1968, Rio Grande's ex-*Chessie* domes were without a regular assignment. Here, at Denver on August 7, 1968, No. 1250 is added to the consist of the *California Zephyr.* (Steve Patterson)

The *Quad Cities Rocket,* with Big Ben in the consist to provide first-class service, has arrived at Rock Island, Illinois, the end of its run. (Mike Schafer)

In August 1972, the Sceneramic Dome is prominent in the consist of CN's *Super Continental* as it rolls westbound by Alberta's Jasper Lake. (Bob Schmidt)

the uniforms of the young hostesses, who replaced the traditional porters as onboard attendants. The staff were nonunion. Meals (prepared off the train and served buffet style) were complimentary. There were cartoons and movies, and live entertainment in the Starlight Lounge, an ex-Santa Fe Big Dome.

The UP domes underwent some modifications. While the dome diners retained their original function, the dome lounges were converted to "Maxi-Dome" coaches, with 20 revenue seats in the dome and 24 on the main level. The space under the dome was given over to a small lounge. The somewhat reconfigured dome coaches also had 20 revenue seats in the dome, with 36 on the main level. Typically, the two versions of the ex-UP coaches alternated in the consist, so no passenger was far from a lounge.

Two of the ex-Santa Fe Big Domes — from the initial order, for the *El Capitan* and *Chicagoan/Kansas Cityan* — became "Starlight Lounges." The balance of the Big Domes were used as coaches, with 51 revenue seats in the dome. (By selling seats in the domes, Auto-Train ran against the virtually universal previous practice of

using domes as nonrevenue space.) The ex-WP coaches had 36 lower-level revenue seats and 12 swivel chairs in the dome, this latter detail a throwback to Santa Fe's Pleasure Domes.

Appreciating the attractiveness of domes, Garfield made them an equipment keynote of his service, which was initially a raging success. Disney World in Orlando, near Sanford, was new and a great draw. Auto-Train Corporation's stock shot up, more than doubling virtually overnight. Long strings of auto-carriers, sleepers, coaches, diners, and lounges — some 25 cars, typically, hauled by General Electric U36Bs — ran sold out much of the time. A third consist, running on alternate days, supplemented the single daily round trip during peak seasons.

After a virtually unbroken run of good years, everything began to unravel in 1976. In that year a pair of derailments caused by overheating brakes saddled the company with legal claims, higher insurance premiums, and smaller (and uneconomical) consists mandated for safety. A Midwest service — Louisville–Sanford, begun in 1974 and combined with

98

Pullman-Standard dome purchased by Illinois Central from Missouri Pacific is seen in March 1968. (John S. Ingles)

At Atlanta in December 1969, the ex-Wabash, ex-N&W dome parlor now owned by the Central of Georgia is in the consist of streamliner *Nancy Hanks II,* about to leave on its six-hour run to Savannah. (Bob Schmidt)

Ex-Wabash, ex-N&W, ex-Central of Georgia, ex-Southern dome in July 1990 serves the Quebec, North Shore & Labrador. This photo is at Ross Bay Junction. (Michael Caramanna)

Amtrak's *Floridian* in 1976 as an economy measure — was terminated in 1977, a flop that had drained the corporation's scarce assets. Gasoline became plentiful, airline and rental-car discounts proliferated, cash grew short, trains were canceled, and internal management problems were alleged.

In September of 1980 the corporation sought protection from creditors under Chapter 11 of the U.S. Bankruptcy Act. Seven months later, on April 30, 1981, *Auto-Train* stopped running — leaving in its wake a weary fleet of undermaintained cars, many of them domes, and a good concept gone awry. The concept Amtrak would pick up two years later, with considerable success. As for the domes, many of them were picked up too. They were among the more attractive items at Auto-Train's liquidation auction, held December 8, 1981, at Sanford, Florida, and many remain active today in private hands. Original owner Union Pacific even bought back a number of them.

Among the UP domes that Auto-Train didn't get in the first place were four dome coaches that went to the Alaska Railroad for service on the Fairbanks–Anchorage train then called the *AuRoRa* — a pun on "ARR," the road's reporting marks, and aurora borealis, or northern lights. Refurbished along with other UP equipment purchased at the same time, the domes entered service, two to a consist, in May 1972. Powered by Electro-Motive Division FP7s dressed, like the coaches, in blue and yellow, this smart streamliner carried a diner and flat-top coaches as well as the domes. Running daily in summer, twice weekly from mid-September to mid-May, the train's 11-plus-hour passage was all or mostly in daylight depending on the season, so the domes were welcome, considering the spectacular nature of the scenery.

Subtraction from ARR's dome fleet occurred in July 1975 when one car was damaged beyond repair in a wreck and subsequently scrapped. On the other hand, a bit less than a decade later, in March and April 1984, major addition would occur when Amtrak leased four ex-*Empire Builder* dome coaches (one GN, one SP&S, two CB&Q) to ARR and, for $11,000 apiece, sold them six ex-*CZ* dome coaches, three Burlington cars (Silver Bridle, Silver Lodge, and Silver Stirrup) and three Rio Grande cars (Silver Colt, Silver Mustang, and Silver Pony).

For a brief period in the mid-1980s, Budd short domes ruled the roost in Alaska, not only on the Fairbanks–Anchorage train but also the Whittier–Fairbanks shuttle, which connects with the Alaska State Ferry. As many as five domes could be spotted in that service. But within two years this Budd armada was once again headed south — the four leased cars returned to Amtrak, the other six sold to Randy Parten, a San Antonio businessman who was trying to start a train service between Denver and Aspen, Colorado.

But even as the Budd short domes departed, private tour operators were adding hundreds of seats under glass to Alaska Railroad's Fairbanks–Anchorage train. Denali National Park, home of Mt. McKinley, was an increasingly attractive tourist destination, especially for the burgeoning numbers of cruise-ship passengers sailing up the Inside Passage from Vancouver to Alaska, and ARR rails would prove the ideal way to get there.

Tour Alaska (now called Princess Tours, an affiliate of Princess Cruises, the "Love Boat" line) was first,

auto-train

Now you can enjoy America's great train and the convenience of your own automobile when traveling to or from Florida.

Domes were an important aspect of what Auto-Train had to sell, so the ex-Santa Fe Big Dome is front and center on this brochure. (Author's Collection)

initiating its *Midnight Sun Express* in 1984 with three ex-Milwaukee Road Super Domes extensively rebuilt at Pacific Car & Foundry at Renton, Washington, at a cost of more than $500,000 per car and named Mt. Foraker, Mt. McKinley, and Mt. Susitna. A fourth car, rebuilt by Tour Alaska itself, entered service in 1987 as Mt. St. Elias. (A fifth car was cannibalized for parts during the conversion of the first three cars and scrapped.)

All passengers were accommodated in the dome area, furnished with plush upholstered seats and oak-trimmed coffee tables. Also on the upper level was a bar. Below was the kitchen, where multicourse meals were prepared from scratch, and a 22-seat dining salon, where they were consumed in elegance — fine china, French stemware, and silver arrayed on white linens.

Tourist business was booming and the 525-mile Alaska Railroad, which in January 1985 had passed from federal to state ownership for $22.3 million, was ready to handle it. In 1988, Princess replaced the Super Domes with "Ultra Domes," bilevel, glass-roofed cars rebuilt from ex-Southern Pacific gallery-type commute coaches. Since these much-admired cars lack forward visibility when coupled together, they aren't traditional domes. (Three of the ex-CMSTP&P cars freed from Alaska service moved to California where, on March 1, 1990, they inaugurated *California Sun Express* service of the Oakland–Los Angeles leg of Amtrak's *Coast Starlight*. After a few months this under-patronized service folded, and the three domes went on to Amtrak's *Auto Train*.)

Meanwhile, enter competitor Westours — an affiliate of Holland America Line, whose ships battle it out with the Princess fleet for supremacy in the Alaska cruise trade. In 1985, Westours assembled a fleet of ten ex-Santa Fe Big Domes, all Auto-Train veterans, eight of them passing through ownership by New York, Susquehanna & Western on the way to Alaska. These cars, configured much like the ex-CMStP&P cars that Princess operated before Ultra Domes, run as the *McKinley Explorer,* carrying names such as Matanuska, Chulitna, Nenana, and Talkeetna. Like the Midnight Sun Express, this operation caters to cruise passengers disembarking at Seward, on the Gulf of Alaska.

Alaska Railroad now was carrying far more passengers in the *Midnight Sun Express* and *McKinley Explorer* domes than in its own cars; still, its equipment remains an important if minority part of the mix, even in terms of domes. Two ARR domes remain in service, one per summer consist. (The third was withdrawn and used as a parts source.) With other ARR cars, the domes were converted to head-end

101

The trifecta of dome styles that runs on the Alaska Railroad — ARR's own ex-UP dome, Westours' ex-Santa Fe Big Domes, and Princess Tours' Ultra Domes — are caught in action in June of 1990 at Riley Creek in Denali Park. (Steve Glischinski)

power in 1982 by General Electric at its Hornell, New York, shops.

In the mid-nineties, the typical summer-season consist for the Fairbanks–Anchorage train included one Alaska Railroad dome, three Princess Tours Ultra Domes, and three to five Big Domes in *McKinley Explorer* service — quite an extraordinary array of seats under glass, beating even the 1950s *Empire Builder* and *California* Zephyr hands down.

Though domes seem to thrive to the north — on the Alaska Railroad, on CP and CN, even on the Quebec, North Shore & Labrador — they never really caught on south of the border. In the watershed year of Amtrak's inauguration, a single Missouri Pacific (later Illinois Central) Budd-built coach went to the Ferrocarril Chihuahua al Pacifico and was named Ciudad de Chihuahua. Subsequently the car was sold to the National Railways of Mexico (Ferrocarril Nacionales de Mexico, or NdeM). Also acquired by NdeM was Silver Planet, a Western Pacific dome observation that had been sold to the Oregon, Pacific & Eastern and subsequently served on the short-lived

Los Angeles commuter train *El Camino*. And in 1987, Union Pacific sold dome coach No. 7006, which it had held for excursion service, to NdeM.

Privately owned domes — first a leased ex-Santa Fe "Pleasure Dome" and, beginning in 1994, an ex-UP dome diner — operate in Mexico on the Sierra Madre Express, a cruise train running to the Copper Canyon. And the South Orient Express, another private train to the Copper Canyon, includes ex-*CZ* dome coaches Silver Stirrup and Silver Colt and dome diner Maroon Bells (rebuilt from a Budd-built Missouri Pacific dome coach) in its consist.

But between the trickle of domes to the south and the freshet to the north there was the vast reservoir of hand-me-down domes in the middle: Amtrak's fleet, a story in itself.

VERY LIKE A DOME

As their name suggests, Princess Tours' four Ultra Domes may be the ultimate dome cars. Standing 17 feet, 5 inches tall, they're more than a foot higher than

On December 28, 1975 ex-Mop, ex-IC Budd-built dome coach (dressed in unadorned stainless steel for the first time in its career) is on the triweekly Vista train en route from Los Mochis to Chihuahua. Operating on the Chuhuahua al Pacifico, the car shows its passengers the scenic wonders of the Copper Canyon region. (William D. Middleton)

any other dome ever built. With their curved panels measuring 84 inches by 72 inches, they have far and away the most upper-level glass of any domes. In basic body shape, however, their most direct ancestors are not any forerunner domes but rather Amtrak's Superliner lounges and their predecessors, the Santa Fe Hi-Level lounges that Budd built in 1956 for the Chicago–Los Angeles *El Capitan.*

Double-deck trains by definition mean no true domes, but Santa Fe's "Top of the Cap" lounges were a fairly good substitute, with curved glass panels contoured to the roof line. Amtrak's "Sightseer" lounges (introduced in 1980) took another step and dramatically expanded the size of the side windows.

But if the Ultra Domes were yet another evolutionary step in this linear development, they were a quantum leap. The four Ultra Domes — named Denali, Gates of the Arctic, Katmai, and Kenai Fjords after

Alaska National Parks — were created from the shells of commute coaches built in 1969 by Pullman-Standard. In turning them into Ultra Domes, 21 inches were added to their height, and immeasurable plush luxury to their interiors, with dining on the lower level and viewing on the upper. (Passage from car to car is on the lower level, as is the case with domes, not the upper level, as aboard Santa Fe's Hi-Levels and Amtrak's Superliners.)

The Ultra Domes cost $3.6 million each, including purchase of the cars from Caltrans. Rebuilding was done in Oregon at Tillamook Railcar Repair, Inc., headed by Thomas G. Radar. The cars operate in twosomes, one car with a kitchen, the other with a large open observation platform.

Seven years after the introduction of the Ultra Domes, Radar provided a similar car in 1995 for Rocky Mountaineer Railtours, a privately operated excursion

Silver Vista, a narrow-gauge sightseeing car inspired by Vista Domes ordered for the *California Zephyr*. (Rio Grande: *Trains* Magazine Collection)

United Aircraft's Turbotrains had some dome credentials, including forward vision through a glass wall separating the engineer's compartment. On May 8, 1971, one week into the Amtrak era, a touring Turbo is keeping company in Santa Fe's Chicago coach yards with a Pleasure Dome from the *Super Chief*. (Jim Heuer)

train through the Canadian Rockies, and an additional one the next year. This dome, marketed as Gold Leaf Service, differs in having both kitchen and open observation platform.

Dome-like characteristics (without the dome's traditional projection above the roof line) were occasionally incorporated in single-level cars as well. Most notable were the trio of Sun Lounge sleepers that Pullman-Standard delivered in 1956 to Seaboard Air Line for its New York–Miami *Silver Meteor*. Named Hollywood Beach, Miami Beach, and Palm Beach, these cars carried five double bedrooms, a buffet, and a distinctive 21-seat lounge with oversized windows and skylights in the roof shoulders. Decor was unique, too: a shell-patterned carpet and driftwood lamps. Renamed Sun View, Sun Beam, and Sun Ray (to free up their original names) after Seaboard's merger with Atlantic Coast Line, the cars continued on the *Meteor* into the Amtrak era.

Other cars akin to domes were the Milwaukee Road's "Skytop" observations, designed by Brooks Stevens and built in 1948 for the *Olympian, Morning,* and *Afternoon Hiawathas*. The six cars for the *Olympian Hi,* Pullman-Standard products, carried eight double bedrooms along with the small but wonderful solarium-style lounge. (After the train's discontinuance, these six cars accompanied the six Super Domes north to CN.) The cars for the *Morning* and *Afternoon Hiawathas*

Seaboard's Sun Lounges on the *Silver Meteor* were the closest thing to domes to enter the Pennsylvania Railroad's tunnels into New York. (Karl Zimmermann)

had 24 parlor seats and a drawing room, along with the small lounge under glass in the round end.

Another car, modest and anomalous, also aspired to domeness. Silver Vista was a diminutive, homemade vehicle, open at the sides with a glass roof, that for a time in the late forties and early fifties trailed the steam-powered Silverton Train over Rio Grande's narrow-gauge rails through Colorado's Animas Canyon. Actually an outfit car rebuilt from the floor up in 1947 to a design created by the railroad's Motive Power and Car Department, the silver-painted Silver Vista no doubt was inspired by the dome cars on order for the *California Zephyr*. (In fact, Burlington rostered a Silver Vista too, a *Twin Zephyr* dome observation also built in 1947.) When the Rio Grande's car perished in 1953 in a fire in the railroad's Alamosa car shops, it was not replaced.

DISTANT DOMES

In its brief but brilliant flowering, the dome-car concept gained such popularity in the American West that hardly a significant passenger railroad running there didn't at least dabble. (Among the mostly secondary players that might have but didn't are Chicago & North Western, Soo Line, Frisco, Katy, and Kansas City Southern.) Canadian roads eventually got the bug too.

Beyond North America, however, the idea never caught on — with a few notable exceptions. One was a fleet of ten Renault-engined diesel-electric motor cars built at Choisy-le-Roi in 1959 for use in the south of France. Called "Panoramiques," these cars were based in Marseilles and ran on services to Clermont-Ferrand, Grenoble, and Digne. Powered by a single diesel engine and two electric traction motors, each car contained 88 seats — 44 in the elevated first-class center section and 22 in each of the main-level second-class sections at the ends, where seating was 2 and 2, but with a jump seat that folded down into the aisle to make five seats across.

Built for the French National Railways — the Société Nationale des Chemins de Fer Francais, or SNCF — these cars wore red and cream livery until their retirement in 1985. A few remain in private ownership today; one, No. X4208, sees regular excursion service under the banner of AGRIVAP, a French organization. The Panoramiques could run in multiple and had the power to haul a trailer, which the X4208 often does when operating today.

A somewhat similar car had been built for service in Italy in 1948, just over a decade before the Panoramiques. Dubbed "Belvedere," this double-ended diesel-electric rail car had a real dome: a "compartimento panoramico sopraelevato." In addition to full forward visibility (which the Panoramiques shared), the Belvedere also had overhead glass. The dome area seated 20; downstairs at both ends were lounges seating 12 each. One end also featured a tiny cocktail car with three stools. Apparently the Belvedere's primary assignment was to run between Torino and Savona, where it connected with Milan-Marseilles Trans-Europ Expresses.

The most famous European dome cars were five built by Wegmann in the early sixties for the *Rheingold* and *Rheinpfeil*, a pair of trains that ran through the valley of Germany's scenic Rhine River. Like the Southern Pacific's home-built dome lounges, these were technically single-level cars, since there was no through passage below the dome.

Though the dome did thrust significantly above the roof line, forward visibility was virtually nonexistent because the seats — 22 in all, reversible and most arranged two-and-one across — sat low in the dome. The triple-layered flat glass panels peaked like a tent, providing both the necessary pass-through headroom and a feeling of bright spaciousness.

At one end on the main level the cars carried two traditional six-seat compartments, with a small secretary's room with desk tucked in beside the stairway to the dome. At the car's other end was a bar with 12 seats. The air-conditioning equipment was beneath the dome, where there was also luggage space, accessed from outside.

The first three cars, delivered in 1962 for the *Rheingold*, carried the train's name in gold on their flanks. (With a history dating back to 1928, this illustrious train ran from Amsterdam and Hook of Holland to Basel, Switzerland, just beyond the German border. When the *Rheingold* became a Trans-Europe Express, it was extended to Geneva.) The following year another pair of cars arrived — for the *Rheinpfeil*, but lettered for Deutsche Bundesbahn (German Federal Railway) rather than for the train. Originally dressed in blue and cream, the cars were repainted in 1967 in Trans-Europe Express red and cream after the trains had joined that international system. In June 1973 the *Rheinpfeil* cars were reassigned to the *Erasmus*.

In May 1976 all five cars were withdrawn from the TEEs and sold to Apfelpfeil, a travel agency that went out of business in 1979. Two years later they were acquired by Reisebüro Mittelthurgau AG, a Swiss travel agency that is actually a subsidiary of the Mittel Thurgau Bahn, one of Switzerland's many private railways. The domes remain in excellent health, frequently venturing out in tour and excursion service.

With its dazzling scenery, Switzerland is certainly an appropriate place for dome cars. Though no true domes were ever built for service there, a number of "near domes" have appeared recently, beginning with the cars on the meter-gauge Montreux-Oberland Bernois's *Panoramic Express*, and later *Superpanoramic* and *Crystal Panoramic Expresses*. Similar panorama cars now run on the *Glacier Express* (operated jointly by the Brig-Visp-Zermatt, Furka Oberalp, and Rhaetian Railway).

The best known dome cars to run outside of North America were probably those introduced on the *Rheingold* in Germany in 1962. (William F. Howes, Jr., Collection)

The mid-nineties saw Swiss Federal Railways take delivery from Schindler Waggon AG of a dozen standard-gauge panorama cars, which run in first-class service on various EuroCity trains. (A much earlier near-dome — the *Glaserne Zug,* or "Glassy Train" — dates from 1935. This German self-propelled car had been preserved and remained in excursion service until it was badly damaged in a fatal collision in 1995.)

Otherwise, domes real or near have been virtually unknown outside of North America. One or more very American-looking cars operated in Russia. In South America, so did the Colombian Railway. That was about the extent of it.

Former Deutsche Bundesbahn dome, now owned by Reisebüro Mittelthurgau, on an excursion in October 1995 (Bob Schmidt)

Preserved Panoramique No. X4208, owned and maintained by AGRIVAP, stops at Chapeauroux on the mountainous Ligne des Cevennes in France with a special operated by Along Different Lines, a British rail tour company, on June 1, 1996. (Richard Pegler, Along Different Lines)

The "Glassy Train" runs between Holzkirchen and Rosenheim on an October 1995 excursion, just two months before its collision with a regional train that had run a red block. (Bob Schmidt)

8

On Amtrak
More Days of Glory

In Amtrak's early years, dome cars were clearly the cream of rolling stock. Their presence automatically lent cachet to any consist.

At its formation in 1971 and shortly afterwards, in keeping with its objective of buying the best cars available from the private railroads, the passenger corporation had acquired a substantial number of domes: 105 cars all told, from among 180 cars presumably on the market. Right away Amtrak grabbed virtually all of the Budd-built domes, reflecting a general strong predisposition toward that builder's Shotwelded products. The Burlington, Great Northern, Northern Pacific, Spokane, Portland & Seattle, Baltimore & Ohio, and Wabash Budd fleets totaled 87 cars, and Amtrak got every one.

Amtrak let Auto-Train make off with 13 of Santa Fe's Budd-built Big Domes. Having been allowed earlier to discontinue its piece of the *California Zephyr,* Western Pacific had no need to join Amtrak, so its seven ex-*CZ* dome coaches also went to Auto-Train, while its Cable Car Room dome and two dome observations went to private owners. Denver & Rio Grande Western declined to join Amtrak, so its six ex-*CZ* domes entered *Rio Grande Zephyr* service and its three ex-*Chessie* cars private ownership. (Amtrak eventually bought one of them.) Amtrak passed on Illinois Central's three ex-Missouri Pacific Budd-built *Eagle* cars (perhaps because of the metal plates installed in place of forward glass) but otherwise took all the Budds (but the Santa Fe Big Domes) that the joining roads had to offer.

Pullman-Standard products were another matter. The only P-S cars Amtrak acquired initially were B&O's two coaches, High Dome and Sky Dome, and

Santa Fe's six "Pleasure Domes." Eventually they would add four of Milwaukee Road's Super Domes (the four the railroad had retained when it sent six to CN); purchased in 1972, the cars did not actually see service until 1975, on the *San Francisco Zephyr* east of Ogden. Though not on the original purchase list, five of Southern Pacific's three-quarter-length home-builts were added immediately — an essential expansion, since these were the only domes that SP would allow on its railroad at the time of the Amtrak start-up.

These were the dome-car pieces of the puzzle that was Amtrak car assignments in the formative years. Generally speaking, Amtrak at first was the great leveler; in train consists, the rich got poorer and the poor got richer. However, this generalization was perhaps less true for domes than other cars. Though domes, in common with most of the other best equipment, had been concentrated on the Western long-hauls, clearances prohibited their transfer to the Eastern trains most deeply in need of help. Domes were shuffled around, however, and quite a few new domeliners were created, particularly among Midwest and West Coast short-hauls.

One dome train that slid right into the Amtrak era virtually unchanged was the *Super Chief,* Nos. 3 and 4, which kept its name and its completely separate and segregated sleeper section, with diner and "Pleasure Dome" car. These domes, often paired with their original dining-car mates, continued on Nos. 3 and 4 right through the decade — long after the train became the *Southwest Limited* when Santa Fe, dismayed by what it perceived as downgrading of standards, withdrew the right to use the copyrighted name "Super Chief."

In dramatic contrast to this history of stability

Both of Burlington's progenitor "pattern domes" — Silver Dome and Silver Castle — survived to wear Amtrak colors. Here, Silver Castle is in at Minneapolis in January 1977. (Steve Glischinski)

stood Nos. 5 and 6, the train that Amtrak briefly called the *California Zephyr* (then the *City of San Francisco, San Francisco Zephyr,* and finally — years later, in the Superliner era, when D&RGW finally threw in the towel on the *Rio Grande Zephyr* and welcomed Amtrak on its railroad — the *California Zephyr* again). While the original *CZ* had been famous for its domes, Amtrak's version of this train limped in that respect.

In 1971 Amtrak inherited the status quo — a triweekly "California Service" west of Denver that traversed the Southern Pacific rather than Western Pacific between Salt Lake City and Oakland — with one critical difference: a Denver–Ogden (instead of Salt Lake) routing on the Union Pacific, because the Rio Grande stayed out of Amtrak. In spite of this scenically inferior route, Amtrak still would have thrown plenty of domes at this train were it not for Southern Pacific's stubbornness regarding standard-profile domes on its lines.

Initially SP held that none but its own home-made low-profile domes, unique among all domes in being essentially single-level cars, could operate anywhere on its system. Thus Amtrak's five ex-SP domes right away became fixtures on Nos. 5 and 6, which was fine as far as it went. Where it went was not quite far enough, however, since the train required six consists in the summer, when it moved from triweekly to daily. (A Chicago–Denver section, descendent of the *Denver Zephyr,* operated daily year-round, initially carrying former Burlington dome coaches and dome buffet lounge-dormitories, the latter either ex-*DZ* or ex-*CZ.*) This meant routine operation of domeless *San Francisco Zephyrs* west of Denver at least one time in six — and in reality more frequently than that, since cars were often bad-ordered.

This situation was perhaps the worst casualty of Amtrak's protracted war with SP over domes. Going back to the days of occasional *CZ* reroutes from WP to SP, when SP insisted the domes not be occupied through tunnels and snowsheds, the railroad had contended that full-height domes could not be operated safely on its mountain routes, with tight curves and tight clearances. In 1973 the railroad made a tiny concession and reversed a previous decision not to accept

An ex-*Twin Zephyr* observation is part of a dome-heavy consist for the westbound *North Coast Hiawatha* as it races through Rondout, Illinois, in 1975. (Mike Schafer)

the three low-profile ex-*Chessie* dome sleepers. (SP required expensive stationary "lean tests" on all domes prior to approval to operate.) Not until the latter 1970s, shortly before the arrival of Superliners (which, paradoxically, the railroad had agreed to operate systemwide as far back as early 1976), did SP open the floodgate to domes.

The Seattle–Oakland–Los Angeles *Coast Starlight* labored under the same constraints as Nos. 5 and 6. This train, triweekly north of Oakland for its first two years, daily afterward, became Amtrak's busiest Western service, achieving this status essentially without benefit of domes. After five domeless years, in the spring of 1976 the *Starlight* received the SP dome lounges that up till then had generally operated on Nos. 5 and 6 (though making cameo appearances on Nos. 11 and 14, the *Starlight*). Only late in its pre-Superliner career did it get the domes it deserved.

If the SP-hosted trains were dome-starved, the Chicago–Seattle *Empire Builder* on Burlington Northern — and occasional running mate *North Coast Hiawatha* on BN's more southerly (ex-Northern Pacific) route to the Northwest — was in comparison dome-stuffed.

This wasn't surprising, since its immediate predecessor — the combined *Empire Builder-North Coast Limited-Twin Zephyr* of 1970 — carried 10 domes (out of 18 passenger cars) on the Chicago–Twin Cities leg of its run.

Initially the *Builder* was to hold down Northwest transcontinental service by itself as a straightforward Chicago–Minneapolis–Seattle run, but politics returned the *North Coast Limited* to the timetable — as a triweekly Minneapolis–Spokane service on the NP, connecting with the *Builder* at both ends — just a month and a half after Amtrak's creation had eliminated it. In the summer of 1971, the combined train east of Minneapolis carried six domes — five BN Budd coaches and a BN Budd full-length lounge.

In the course of the 1970s Amtrak's Northwest service continued to evolve, first with the *North Coast Limited's* extension east to Chicago (and renaming to "North Coast Hiawatha," reflecting the new duality of its role), later west to Seattle. Frequency went from triweekly to daily in summer. But in 1979 the train was axed entirely, victim of what had been the most drastic Amtrak cutbacks until the 1995 pruning. Also in 1979, in October, the dome era for the *Empire Builder*

The St. Louis-bound *Abraham Lincoln* carries an ex-*Kansas City Zephyr* observation through Joliet, Illinois. (Mike Schafer)

began to slip away, as the train became the first to receive Superliner consists, two initially.

In the meantime, however, the two Northwest transcons had sported some notable domes. During one early period the *North Coast Hi* boasted two pairs of elegant ex-*Zephyr* dome observations: the *DZ* pair, parlors Silver Chateau and Silver Veranda, between Chicago and Minneapolis, which gave way to ex-*CZ* sleeper-lounges west of there. Before long, however, these ex-*CZ* observations were transferred to the Chicago–Houston *Texas Chief*; later replacements on the *Builder* were ex-*CZ* "Cable Car Room" buffet-lounge dormitory cars. After that, ex-*Twin Zephyr* dome parlor-observations Silver View and Silver Vista (along with the essentially identical ex-Wabash *Blue Bird* obs) often appeared, between stints on the Portland–Seattle *Mount Rainier* and *Puget Sound* or the Seattle–Vancouver *International*. The two *Twin Zephyr* cars, rebuilt at Autoliner Corporation with lounge chairs and tables in place of parlor seats, ran on the Chicago–St. Louis *Prairie State* and Chicago–Miami *Floridian* before being based in Seattle toward the end of their brief Amtrak lives, which concluded prematurely in 1976 because of chronic mechanical problems.

In addition to these feature cars, the *North Coast Hi* typically carried two or more dome coaches and, for a time, a "Lounge in the Sky" dome sleeper from predecessor *North Coast Limited*. The *Empire Builder* likewise carried multiple dome coaches and a "Lounge in the Sky" sleeper, along with the full-length dome lounges built for that train in 1955.

Amtrak's *Texas Chief* featured Santa Fe's "Big Dome" lounges for the first summer season — until September 1971, when Auto-Train snapped up all but one of the fleet of 14. Later ex-BN dome coaches ran in tandem with flat-top lounges, and still later the *CZ* observations came over from the *North Coast Hi*. In 1975, the train — now called the *Lone Star*, since Santa Fe pulled back the name Texas Chief along with Super Chief — included ex-*North Coast Limited* dome sleepers between stints on the *Panama Limited* and the *Empire Builder*. Then the train, which always had included ex-Santa Fe Hi-Level coaches, went domeless. In 1979 it became another casualty of the train-offs.

Alert to their attractiveness, Amtrak's consist planners thinned out domes where they appeared in profusion and transplanted the cuttings to other (often lesser) trains across the system. In fact, the dome bounty — largely in the form of the prolific ex-BN fleet of coaches and sleepers — was shared on virtually every route with adequate clearances.

The overnight Chicago–New Orleans *Panama Limited* of Illinois Central heritage carried a dome coach and/or dome sleeper for a time, as did the Chicago–Carbondale, Illinois, *Shawnee* — briefly, in 1972. (IC's *Panama* had been domeless, though its

111

daylight running-mate, the *City of New Orleans,* had carried ex-Missouri Pacific domes in its last few years. Amtrak passed up those cars and, in fact, bought no cars of any kind from IC.) Fast becoming one of the dogs of the Amtrak system, the train was domeless by 1975.

Another of Amtrak's less sterling performers was the Chicago–Washington/Newport News *James Whitcomb Riley* — a combination of Penn Central's Chicago–Cincinnati *Riley* and Chesapeake & Ohio's *George Washington* east of there. This train's Newport News section generally carried a dome coach from Chicago. (At times, head-end cars aside, the dome *was* the Newport News section.) In 1975 the *Riley* began running combined with the politically inspired *Mountaineer,* an "experimental train" (two of which at that time were mandated annually by Congress) which split off from the *Riley* at Russell, Kentucky (east of Cincinnati), to run over Norfolk & Western rails to tidewater at Norfolk. While it lasted (which was just two years), the train carried a dome coach.

Among the cars assigned were the P-S pair from B&O, High Dome and Sky Dome. Previous to their appearance on the *Mountaineer,* they had been half the consist of another political boondoggle: the Washington–Parkersburg, West Virginia, *West Virginian,* porked into being by Harley Staggers, chairman of the House Commerce Committee. Interesting for their uniqueness but essentially unattractive with their squat profile, this pair of cars was out of Amtrak service by 1976.

Before that, they'd appeared briefly in yet another of Amtrak's troubled trains: the *Floridian,* which initially served both St. Petersburg and Miami from Chicago. Its first assigned domes in Amtrak operation were also B&O veterans: the trio of dome sleepers built for *Chessie* and owned at the end by Seaboard Coast Line. These were replaced by the other sleeper domes — former *North Coast Limited* cars, some of which had appeared in winter lease in the 1960s in the consists of the Floridian's predecessors *City of Miami* and *South Wind.* After that came dome coaches, including the B&O cars.

The *Miamian, West Virginian, Riley,* and *Mountaineer* were among the few trains to carry domes into the eastern reaches of Amtrak. Another was the New York–Montreal *Adirondack,* arguably the East's most scenic service, which had a brief but flamboyant dome-car era. This train was a so-called 403(b), or state-supported, service, in which New York, Amtrak, and the Delaware & Hudson Railway made an uneasy triumvirate. What set the train apart from literally every other train Amtrak has ever fielded was the desire by the operating railroad to be the active, visible partner.

With Carl B. Sterzing, the railroad's president, leading the way, D&H insisted on a train of its own cars (refurbished at state expense), decked out in its own handsome yellow, blue, and gray livery, pulled by its own last-of-their-kind Alco PA diesels. When the train was inaugurated in August 1974 and for some months thereafter, until D&H's own diner-lounges were ready, a pair of "Skyline" dome coach-buffet lounges were leased from Canadian Pacific to provide meal service. After these cars were returned to CP, the train was domeless for some months until September 1975, when Amtrak added Budd dome coaches (ex-*Blue Bird*) from its own pool.

The blood between D&H and Amtrak was bad indeed, and the two sides warred incessantly over issues of maintenance and identity. It's said that D&H even dressed those Amtrak domes in D&H colors — briefly. Whose train was this anyway? On March 1, 1977, Amtrak swept away the whole issue — and all of D&H's equipment, and the dome cars too — by assigning Turboliners to the *Adirondack.*

In the Midwest, a number of short-haul, daylight schedules had moments as domeliners. A 403(b) service like the *Adirondack,* the Chicago–West Quincy, Illinois, *Illinois Zephyr* was typically stocked with ex-Chicago & North Western bilevel cars, but domes were in the picture during an extended period of operation with single-level cars in the mid-1970s. The most interesting of the domes assigned was Linoma, the ex-*Chessie,* ex-Rio Grande coach-buffet lounge-observation first leased and then purchased by Amtrak. Linoma earlier had seen service on the *Pacific International* and *Inter-American* and later did a lengthy stint on the *San Francisco Zephyr* before taking early retirement in 1976 — a common fate for Amtrak's nonstandard domes.

One notable innovation in Amtrak's early months was the inauguration of St. Louis–Milwaukee through service, an experiment that lasted two years and yielded a version of Gulf, Mobile & Ohio's St. Louis–Chicago *Abe Lincoln* that was a truly exceptional daylight train, replete with diner, dome, and observation. Dome parlor-observations Silver Terrace and Silver Tower (ex-*Kansas City Zephyr*) ran briefly, before being replaced by flat-top parlor-observations (used on Great Northern's *International*). Later, running mate *Prairie State* was assigned a refurbished Silver Tower, along with Silver View and Silver Vista (ex-*Twin Zephyr*). Then October 1973 saw French-built Turboliners bump these conventional dome-carrying consists into (temporary) oblivion, just as their Rohr-built Turbo cousins would the domed *Adirondack* four

In November 1972 in a wet snow at Bloomington, Illinois, the consist of the westbound *Prairie State* is trailed by dome observation Linoma, built some 25 years earlier for C&O. (Bob Schmidt)

At Thurmond, West Virginia, an ex-Great Northern Great Dome is deadheading eastbound on the Cardinal, fresh from refurbishing and conversion to head-end-power at Amtrak's Beech Grove Shops and destined for service on the *Auto Train*. (Jim Boyd)

years later. But *Abe* did have another go as a conventional train beginning in 1976, with dome parlor-buffet lounge-observation Silver Chateau (ex-*Denver Zephyr*) carrying the markers.

The kiss of death for most Amtrak domes was the corporation's decision to make double-deck Superliners — lineal descendants of Santa Fe's "Hi-Level" cars inaugurated in 1956 on the all-coach *El Capitan* — the standard equipment in the West. These cars, delivered from 1978 through 1981 (with a new generation of Superliner II cars coming in 1994 and 1995), eventually spelled the end for domes in all of their traditional assignments: the *Empire Builder*, the *San Francisco Zephyr*, the *Southwest Limited*. The advent of head-end-powered Amfleet had already bumped the steam-heated dome fleet off shorter runs.

But just when it looked as though Amtrak had turned its back completely on domes, the passenger corporation initiated a small program in the mid-1980s to convert a few domes to head-end power, which by then was the system-wide mode of electric generation and heat. The HEP domes were slated primarily for the Virginia-to-Florida *Auto Train*, but they also saw service on other routes where non-Superliner equipment was assigned and clearances permitted: the Washington–Chicago *Capitol Limited* and Chicago–New Orleans *City of New Orleans* — a renaming of the *Panama Limited*. All domes upgraded in this project, plus an additional pool held for possible future conversion but never tapped, were Budd products.

At its Beech Grove Shops in Indianapolis, Amtrak in 1985 rebuilt three former *Empire Builder* full-length domes for *Auto Train* service: 9300, Ocean View; 9301, Mountain View; and 9302, River View. (These are their new numbers.) A fourth car, Prairie View, remained on the Amtrak roster for a time as a candidate for future rebuilding, then eventually was sold to Burlington Northern. BN plans to rebuild the car for executive train consists, where sister Glacier View has served for more than a decade.

In 1983–84 a dozen short dome coaches had been converted to head-end power and renumbered

9400–9411 when they joined the "Heritage Fleet," as Amtrak called its older, rebuilt equipment. They operated interchangeably on all of Amtrak's dome trains, except that assignment to the *Auto Train* required installation of freight brake valves (initially provided for Nos. 9404, 9407, and 9409), since all *Auto Train* cars are so equipped. Nine of these short domes had been built for the *North Coast Limited* and three for the *Empire Builder*. Another 15 similar cars were initially held in a pool for possible conversion: two cars from the *Denver Zephyr*, nine from the *Empire Builder*, two from the *North Coast Limited*, and two from the *Blue Bird*.

None of these 15 were ever rebuilt by Amtrak. Ditto the more exotic cars in Amtrak's "mothball fleet" of domes: four former *North Coast Limited* sleepers and five ex-Burlington observation lounges: Silver Terrace and Silver Tower from the *Kansas City Zephyr*, Silver Veranda from the *Denver Zephyr*, and Silver Penthouse from the *California Zephyr*. After being held for a time, these cars were subsequently sold — with Silver Veranda and Silver Penthouse, like Prairie View, going to BN.

Both the *Capitol Limited* and the *City of New Orleans* are trains with dome heritage, of course. The *Cap* was a domeliner from 1950 virtually up to its (temporary, as it turned out) discontinuance at Amtrak's inception, and the *City* in the late sixties carried domes purchased from Missouri Pacific and Texas & Pacific.

Then in 1994, the golden anniversary year of Cyrus Osborn's brainstorm, Superliners began elbowing in again. Delivery of a second round of the double-deck cars — Superliner IIs — allowed the conversion of first the *City of New Orleans* (on May 1) and then the *Capitol Limited* (on October 30) to Superliner trains, shunting aside the domes, or at least freeing them for reassignment. Beginning May 1, they began running on the Chicago–Albany segment of the *Lake Shore Limited*.

Not long afterward the train and its dome car attracted unwanted attention by derailing at Batavia, New York. This was a spectacular (though nonfatal) accident, and the greatest spectacle was the dome coach lying with its dome area mangled. The car went off the Amtrak roster as a total loss. So strong was the market for dome cars, however, that an individual purchased the derelict car, hoping to combine it with another wreck-damaged dome and create a sound car from parts of two shattered ones.

As 1995 began, Amtrak's only dome operations were the *Lake Shore* and *Auto Train*, with the latter being something of a dome showcase. To the Budd short and full-length domes in operation since 1985, the carrier had added full-length "Starlight" dome diners for sleeping-car passengers. To provide this service, Amtrak acquired a trio of former Milwaukee Road Super Domes from Princess Tours and reconfigured them for dining in the dome area, adding a dumb-waiter and tinted dome glass. (These much-traveled cars were among the six sold to Canadian National; their last pre-Amtrak assignment was on the short-lived *California Sun Express*.)

But Amtrak was not destined to be a participant when the Silver Dome car celebrated its fiftieth birthday in July 1995. In fact, Amtrak domes would come up a half-year short, failing to make it out of January. First *Auto Train* fell to Superliners, which left the *Lake Shore* as Amtrak's only domeliner. But money was brutally tight as Amtrak began what was to be a year of budget and service cuts, and this lingering dome operation seemed an unnecessary and unproductive luxury. Thus Amtrak's dome-car era finally came to a close when the westbound *Lake Shore Limited* arrived at Chicago Union Station's bumping post on January 25, 1995.

Private Domes
Yesterday's Trains *for* Tomorrow

As dome cars dwindled to a precious few on Amtrak, private owners, tourist- and dinner-train operators, and even freight railroads both large and small have been stalwart in keeping these cars rolling fifty and more years after Osborn dreamed them up. The roster of domes in these services is long, diverse, and fluid. New operations spring up and old ones fold, sometimes most unexpectedly, and domes in private ownership are constantly changing hands.

The dinner train is a curious phenomenon born in the mid-1980s, fueled presumably by nostalgia for the glamour of dining on rails in the golden age of the passenger train. Dinner trains have been an up-and-down business, with many brave beginnings — and quite a number of failures as well.

In any case, domes have played a significant role in the decade of dinner trains, and a number of dinner trains featured domes in the 1990s. These included the Stillwater-based *Minnesota Zephyr*, with a rare pair: Southern Pacific's home-built three-quarter length No. 3604, now called Grand Dome, and a Pullman-Standard short dome, ex-Missouri Pacific No. 894, now named St. Croix. Nashville's *Broadway Dinner Train*, which for years has operated a "Pleasure Dome" of Santa Fe *Super Chief* heritage, added to its roster Silver Stream, a *Twin Zephyrs* dome coach.

In the Pacific Northwest, the *Spirit of Washington* dinner train, subsequently shipped north to run out of Vancouver on BC Rail as the *Pacific Starlight Dinner Train*, also had a "Pleasure Dome" (which it had named City of Seattle), along with an ex-Union Pacific dome diner (wearing fluted stainless below its windows and named Mt. Rainier) and an ex-Milwaukee Super Dome (City of Renton).

In the generally domeless East, Hyannis, Massachusetts-based Cape Cod Railroad has an ex-Wabash *Blue Bird* dome coach in excursion service. In addition, an ex-*Empire Builder* short dome is on the property, and plans call for its use in the line's dinner-train consist, with the main-floor short end converted to a lounge and the long end to a dining area. The EnterTRAINment Line's dinner train, running out of Union Bridge, Maryland, used an ex-UP dome diner for a time, until it was sold to become part of the *Sierra Madre Express*, a private train offering excursions to Mexico's Copper Canyon.

Ex-UP domes seemingly are everywhere, so it's not surprising that some of the most spectacular and startling terminations among dinner and excursion trains have involved these cars. Consider Milwaukee-based Scenic Rail Dining, one of the notable successes early in the dinner train era. Outstandingly elegant in blue, yellow, and gray livery, all but the kitchen car in this train's four-car consist were ex-UP domes: a diner, a coach (converted for dining), and an observation-lounge that carried a drumhead and had its rear windows unblocked.

The cars were beautifully renovated at Bill Gardner's Northern Rail Car Corporation in Cudahy, Wisconsin, where numerous other domes have since been reborn into new careers. Scenic Rail Dining, another Gardner enterprise, was under wife Dianne's supervision. The train's 76-mile round-trips from Milwaukee to Horicon were over the rails of Wisconsin & Southern — a short line that is also part of the Gardner empire.

Scenic Rail Dining was getting rave reviews and, apparently, was sold out for months ahead when, with-

116

The *Minnesota Zephyr* dinner train carries an ex-SP home-built. (Karl Zimmermann)

out warning in October 1990, it simply stopped. The three domes and kitchen car were shipped to California to be part of Transcisco Tours' *Sierra 49er Express,* a luxury "cruise train" that was to run from the San Francisco Bay Area to Reno and Lake Tahoe. Scuttlebutt was that Transcisco made an offer simply too good for Gardner to refuse.

The Transcisco saga turned out to be a sad one. To start with, the cars that had looked so stylish in SRD livery were given a garish and misguided scarlet and blue scheme for Transcisco service. (Nor could the boxy SD45s that headed the Transcisco consist hold a candle to the sleek E9 that had done the honors for SRD.) In addition to the SRD cars, the *Sierra 49er Express* consist would include a pair of Southern Pacific gallery commute coaches rebuilt as "Deluxe Class" cars. (This was actually a second-class accommodation, with "Luxury Dome Class" being first.) There was also a lounge and sleeper leased from the recently defunct *American European Express,* and an ex-Santa Fe coach used as an entertainment car. This last was moved from the San Antonio-based *Texan Dining Train;* in June 1990 Transcisco had bought this operation from the group of local investors who founded it.

Operating twice weekly over the 285-mile route from San Jose via Oakland to Truckee (for Lake Tahoe) and Reno, the *Sierra 49er Express* was sold as a three-day, two-night package that included rail transportation, on-board meals, and hotel accommodations, plus discounts on rental cars, restaurants, and ski-lift tickets. Prices were surprisingly reasonable, particularly for the weekday package — this in the face of substantial start-up costs. But Transcisco Tours was part of Transcisco Industries, a large firm involved in freight-car maintenance and retrofitting, and one that apparently wasn't averse to major spending.

After some demonstration trips beginning in December 1990, the *Sierra 49er Express* made its official inaugural run on January 11, 1991. Hoped-for business levels never developed, however, with patronage reported at roughly half of the 400 per trip that had been projected. After barely three months of operation, Transcisco threw in the towel, suspending service with the April 26–28 round trip. Thus the *Sierra 49er Express* followed close on the markers of the *American European Express* and the *California Sun Express,* highballing into luxury-train oblivion.

Transcisco's other operation, the *Texan Dining Train,* would go the same route. The train had begun operation in August 1988 under the auspices of Texas

In June 1988, the Wyoming Colorado Railroad's excursion train includes *CZ* veterans Silver Pony and Silver Colt as it runs along Lake Owen in the Medicine Bow National Forest. (Roger Cook)

Southern, a group of investors who spent $2.5 million to restore an A-B-A set of ex-U.S. Steel F7s (which once served the Atlantic City Mine railroad in Wyoming) and various passenger cars. These included a trio of domes: ex-Western Pacific Silver Feather, a coach converted for dome dining, with a main-level lounge; an ex-Missouri Pacific *Colorado Eagle* dome coach, also converted for dining; and an ex-*Super Chief* "Pleasure Dome."

The restoration work was of high quality, and unusually respectful of the cars' heritage. And additional domes were acquired with the idea of supplementing the consist: ex-*California Zephyr* observation Silver Horizon and *Twin Zephyrs* coach Silver Vision. But this train too had a limited future, eventually going down under the Transcisco Tours banner.

A dome-toting Lone Star State train that proved to have more staying power was the Galveston–Houston

Texas Limited, not a dinner train but a weekend excursion that began operating between those cities in late summer of 1989. Most of the equipment in this service is leased from Randy Parten's Denver Railway Car Company. (Parten, a San Antonio businessman, was one of the founders of the Texan Dining Train and also CEO of the stillborn Roaring Fork Railroad, which was to run from Denver to Aspen). The leased cars include Silver Stirrup, an ex-*CZ* dome coach that did time in Alaska.

Other ex-Alaska Railroad *Zephyr* cars in the Roaring Fork stable have run on the excursions of the Wyoming Colorado Railroad, which began in 1987 to operate 95 miles of line between Laramie, Wyoming, and Walden, Colorado — most of what had been the UP's Coalmont Branch. Spiffy passenger consists, hauled by equally spiffy pair of FP7As (also ARR veterans, leased from Mountain Diesel Transportation),

In April 1994, Union Pacific ran a "Domeliner" excursion with its repatriated dome cars. (Steve Glischinski)

included a pair of ex-Denver & Rio Grande Western *CZ* coaches: Silver Pony and Silver Colt. (Freight operations on the line concluded in July 1994; excursions continued for a time, though without the ex-*CZ* domes.) Denver Rail Car subsequently used Silver Colt, along with ex-*CZ* fleetmate Silver Stirrup and an ex-Missouri Pacific coach (converted for dining and named Maroon Bells) on its *South Orient Express* excursions to Mexico's Copper Canyon.

Other former *Zephyr* cars are at the heart of one of the newest excursion operations: Branson Scenic Railway, which began running on July 31, 1993. The line offers 42-mile round trips into the Ozark Mountains on two different routes from Branson, Missouri, which has blossomed as a new country music capital. Stars have built theaters there, 36 all told, which combine with three theme parks to make this once-tiny village a hot destination. Branson Scenic uses former *CZ* observation Silver Solarium and *Kansas City Zephyr/American Royal Zephyr* chair-dormitory-buffet lounge Silver Garden, along with the ex-*Super Chief* "Pleasure Dome" Plaza Santa Fe. (The Santa Fe car has replaced ex-*CZ* coach Silver Palace, the third car when service was begun.)

The ebb and flow of domes is continual. While Branson Scenic represents a bright beginning, other dome short stories in this era of private ownership have had abrupt, unhappy endings, like the Transcisco trains. The late, lamented New Georgia Railroad operating in and around Atlanta, for instance, ran UP dome-coach 7000 until the demise of the railroad in 1994.

Union Pacific and its relation to its own cars provide perhaps the most interesting and instructive saga of dome cars in the 1990s. Back in 1971, UP unloaded most of its 40 ACF and P-S domes: 33 to Auto-Train, four to the Alaska Railroad, and one, a diner, as a donation to the National Railway Museum in Green Bay, Wisconsin. For special train service it kept only dome coach No. 7006 (subsequently sold, in January 1987, to the National Railways of Mexico) and dome lounge No. 9004, which UP named Harriman and restricted to business-train service. Before long UP reacquired sister car 9005 from Auto-Train, which had never been painted or renumbered. 9005 became the Walter Dean and was also restricted to executive use.

Some two decades after deaccessioning its dome fleet, however, UP has done some significant reaccessioning. Recognizing the public-relations value of passenger excursions — whether behind steam or its elegant lash-up of Armour-yellow E-units — UP has in recent years repatriated six additional domes, all once owned by Auto-Train, for excursion and business-train

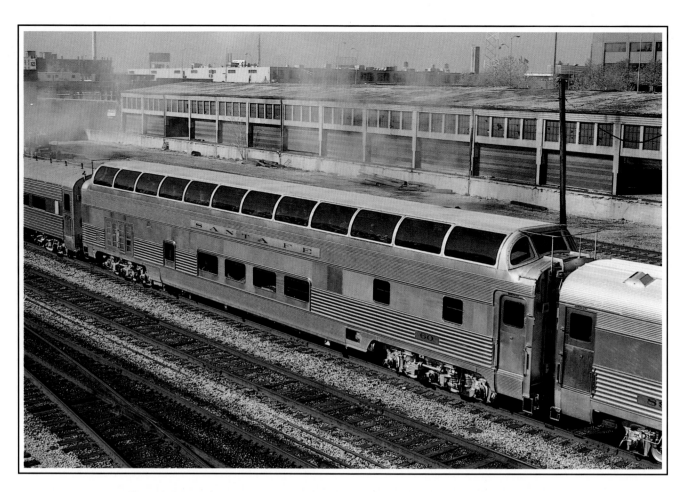

At Chicago, Santa Fe's Big Dome No. 60 is in the consist of a May 1987 Operation Lifesaver special. (Mike Blaszak)

service. Having adopted the convention of naming its excursion fleet (domed or otherwise) for heritage passenger trains — its own or merger partner Missouri Pacific's — the railroad now rosters dome coaches Nos. 7001 Columbine, 7012 (originally 7011) Missouri River Eagle, and 7015 Challenger; dome diners Nos. 8004 Colorado Eagle and 8008 City of Portland; and dome lounge No. 9009 City of San Francisco.

The last three reacquisitions were the trio of domes that once wore Scenic Rail Dining blue, yellow, and gray and then Transcisco's ghastly scheme. From there they went to Paw Paw, Michigan-based Kalamazoo, Lake Shore & Chicago Railroad for service on the *Wine Country Dinner Train*. After that they were readied for return to UP service and once more cloaked in Armour yellow, red, and gray, no doubt the most elegant of their many garbs, at Northern Rail Car, where they already had a good deal of history.

Union Pacific is far from the only Class 1 railroad to roster domes in the post-private-passenger era. Santa Fe's "Big Dome" No. 506, the one that didn't go to Auto-Train, remains a frequent participant in com-

pany specials, now designated No. 60. In 1988 Conrail acquired sister car No. 552 (now CR 55) for its business train. In the 1980's, Chicago & North Western — not previously a dome owner — purchased ex-Milwaukee Road Super Dome No. 53 (later a Canadian National car) from the Mid-Continent Railway Museum for use in its inspection train. To match the rest of the consist, the dome, which C&NW named Powder River, was repainted in the original 400 livery: yellow, green, and black.

Burlington Northern, which reacquired ex-Great Northern Glacier View from Amtrak in 1983 (in trade for three baggage cars) and rebuilt it into a track inspection car, now has some additional domes on the property pending rebuilding: coach Silver Ranch, parlor-observation Silver Veranda, and sleeper observation Silver Penthouse, all ex-CB&Q, and Great Northern's full-length Prairie View, sister to Glacier View.

California, a glamorously renovated dome sleeper tricked out in "Grande Gold," with Rio Grande markings, began life as a Spokane, Portland & Seattle car built for the North Coast Limited. The car passed through Amtrak service and private ownership before Denver & Rio Grande Western (actually parent Ansco Investments) bought it and restored it for executive and charter service. Though owned by parent company Southern Pacific since the merger, the car has retained its D&RGW livery. Hedging its heritage is the former *CZ* coach Silver Lariat, ex-CB&Q, now in private ownership. It carries a removable "Southern Pacific" overlay on its letterboard when chartered by SP or running in excursion service over SP rails.

Domes aren't only on the big Class 1 roads either. Aberdeen, Carolina & Western in 1994 acquired ex-CB&Q *Denver Zephyr* coach Silver Brand. New York, Susquehanna & Western rosters domes, including former *Twin Zephyrs* observation Silver View, acquired from Amtrak. The Susquehanna also bought a large number of domes from Auto-Train after that operator's demise: eight ex-Santa Fe "Big Domes" and a pair of ex-UP domes — one coach and one lounge. Except one consumed in a fire set by vandals, all the Santa Fe cars were subsequently sold to Westours, where they currently form the bulk of the company's Alaska fleet. The UP coach was sold to Pennsylvania's Reading & Northern, where — in dark green dress tricked out in gold, as No. 3, Catawissa — it runs in excursion service. The UP lounge wears NYS&W wine red, running in executive and excursion service as theater-observation car 509.

In the Midwest, Escanaba & Lake Superior rosters an ex-Milwaukee Super Dome that may be returned to service. Wisconsin & Southern's private train, resplendent in silver and red livery, includes a pair of ex-UP dome lounges from the AT group: Nos. 9003, and 9007, named Northern Sky and Northern View. ("Northern Sky" has replaced "Wisconsin Central" on the car's letterboard, reflecting its private ownership.)

Wisconsin Central acquired ex-UP/AT dome lounge Trempeleau River with its 1993 purchase of Green Bay & Western. And WC is also home to Sierra Hotel, a privately owned luxury dome that the railroad leases for business trips. This car, which began life as a Burlington dome lounge-dormitory in *CZ* service, has had an open observation platform added.

Sierra Hotel is one of many domes that qualify as "PVs," or private cars. ("PV" means "private varnish," a term stemming from the era when luxury passenger car exteriors as well as interiors were made of varnished wood.) By definition, a car not railroad-owned is privately owned. Some owners keep PVs strictly for their own use, others strictly or primarily for charter; many straddle these two camps. For most owners their cars are a hobby, but for some they're a business.

Susquehanna's ex-UP dome lounge, rebuilt as a theater/inspection car, is in an excursion consist approaching Stockholm, New Jersey. (Roger Cook)

Some own groups of cars, like the fleet — including the ex-Zephyr domes acquired from the Alaska Railroad in October 1986 — that Randy Parten assembled for the never-to-be Roaring Fork Railroad.

By 1994 roughly 80 privately owned domes had been assigned either permanent or temporary numbers by Amtrak for movement, though many fewer meet Amtrak's current operational requirements. (In this total are the Alaska fleets of Westours and Princess Tours, an indication of just how gray the area of "private ownership" can be.) At the American Association of Private Railroad Car Owners' 1993 convention in Sacramento, for example, seven of the 44 member-owned cars in attendance were domes: Plaza Santa Fe (a Santa Fe "Pleasure Dome"), Native Son and Northern Sky (originally UP dome lounges), Columbia River (UP dome diner), Silver Lookout (*CZ* observation), Silver Lariat (*CZ* coach), and Sierra Hotel. These are among the more active of the private domes.

A few railfan groups own domes. Examples include the Collis P. Huntington Chapter of the National Railway Historical Society in West Virginia with its ex-UP dome coach and Heart of Dixie Chapter in Birmingham with an ex-Missouri Pacific Budd dome coach. In 1994, the Chesapeake & Ohio Historical

In May 1989, C&NW's Powder River is reflected in the still waters of Turtle Creek on a Proviso–Janesville trip. (Bruce C. Nelson)

Powder River's interior, stocked for entertaining (Mike Schafer)

Society was given one of the dome observations built for the Chessie.

Privately owned domes sometimes appear in excursion trains operated by such groups. In the Huntington Chapter's annual *New River Train,* for instance, the well-traveled Moonlight Dome has run in recent years, along with an ex-CMStP&P Super Dome and, of course, the club's own ex-UP dome, which was joined in 1994 by a sister car, property of St. Louis Car Company.

A review of the roster of extant dome cars in the mid-1990s leads to one inescapable conclusion: the staying power of these charismatic cars has been remarkable, especially considering that the oldest were nearing age 50 and even the youngest were close to 40. Of the grand total of 236 dome cars built for service in North America, more than 200 survived

122

Reading & Northern's ex-Union Pacific dome coach, now named Catawissa, is in excursion service at Jim Thorpe, Pennsylvania, in October 1994. (Karl Zimmermann)

through 1994. Of the 31 that had been scrapped, all but a small handful were cut up only after being irrevocably damaged by wreck or fire. Most of the exceptions were cars cannibalized for parts, particularly by Auto-Train.

In many cases, whole fleets survive intact or nearly so: all six of Santa Fe's "Pleasure Domes," for instance, and 12 of 14 of its "Big Domes"; all but one of the Empire Builder's six full-length domes, and all but one of Milwaukee's ten. Of the 22 dome coaches and dome sleepers built for the *North Coast Limited,* all but one survive. Of the 53 Silver-prefix cars built for *Zephyr* service, 46 survive.

The one notable exception to this generalization is the four domes built for the General Motors *Train of Tomorrow* and later operated by the Union Pacific. All were sent to scrap yards in the sixties, and three — Star Dust, Sky View, and Dream Cloud — were cut up. Surprisingly, the fourth — dome-observation lounge Moon Glow, retired in November 1964 — somehow survived. After languishing unremarked (and of course deteriorating dramatically) in a Pocatello, Idaho, scrap yard, this car was rescued in 1990 by the Ogden Union Station Museum in Utah. Currently work is under way to restore the car.

Also surviving is another chief symbol of dome-car

history: Silver Dome, the first working out in metal of the thumbnail sketches that Cy Osborn made that night in 1944 at the Hotel Utah. The car, at the Mad River and NKP Railroad Museum in Bellvue, Ohio, is currently under restoration. Perhaps surprisingly, considering its somewhat jury-rigged nature, the car was not only purchased by Amtrak but had a lengthy service life, lingering long enough to be snatched up for preservation. This was also true of CB&Q's other "pattern dome," Silver Castle, which survives in private ownership in Kansas City and is operable.

Other museums house domes. Green Bay's National Railway Museum has the dome diner UP gave it in 1971. The car, still wearing UP Armour yellow dress and now named Edward Harriman, is on indoor display. Tennessee Valley Railroad in Chattanooga has an ex-C&O, ex-D&RGW dome coach-observation-lounge. On the museum property of the Railway Exposition Company at Covington, Kentucky, are a former Wabash *Blue Bird* coach as well as the former CMStP&P full-length dome used in the *New River Train.* The latter has been returned to the handsome orange and maroon livery it wore when delivered in 1952. These cars operate in charter service.

Before Amtrak's head-end-power requirements, so did Silver Crescent, the former *CZ* observation that

In August 1994, Wisconsin & Southern owner William Gardner brought the short line's private train west with 15 guests and a crew of eight to tour Glacier Park. Here the train nears Marias Pass, Montana. (Bill Taylor)

had been lovingly and accurately restored at Miami's Gold Coast Railroad Museum. Indicative of the unusual concern for authenticity shown at the museum was the replacement of the windshield wipers that Budd provided on the front and rear dome windows of the *CZ* domes.

Wipers on the flanking windows were driven by motors tucked under the roofline, while on the center window the motor was in a box above. The motors were powered by air drawn from the train line and controlled by the car's porter, using switches hidden away on the forward bulkhead of the under-dome cocktail lounge and by the writing desk in the lounge. In the restoration, which returned the wipers to working condition, museum personnel used original Budd blueprints.

Apparently the wipers lasted only a few months in service before being abandoned and removed, having proved impractical in a number of ways. For one thing,

the rotary washer used to clean the *CZ* en route at Denver pulled at them. And the wipers apparently did more to smear than to clear the rich, oily stew of diesel sludge and spattered bugs that routinely forms on forward dome windows. So wipers, which seem never again to have been tried on dome cars, were the kind of idea that sounds good in theory but flunks the test of practicality.

Silver Crescent's splendid restoration turned out to be as tenuous as the windshield wipers when, in August of 1992, Hurricane Andrew slashed across southern Florida, devastating the museum and causing serious structural and water damage to the *CZ* dome. Eventually *Silver Crescent* was sent to Kasten Rail Car for repairs, including replacement of damaged fluting on the car's windward flank and installation of new carpeting, a reproduction of the original fern pattern. By early 1995 this classic Vista-Dome was once more a museum piece of integrity and beauty.

Roster: The Dome Cars of North America

This roster, organized by original owning railroad, tracks initial train assignments and subsequent sales to Class 1 railroads for revenue service only. Years listed are when cars were delivered. Second numbers for Amtrak and VIA cars indicate conversion to head-end power.

Abbreviations: ACF = American Car & Foundry; ARR = Alaska Railroad; A-T = Auto-Train; B&O = Baltimore & Ohio Railroad; Budd = The Budd Company; CB&Q = Chicago, Burlington & Quincy Railroad; CHP = Chihuahua Pacific Railway; CN = Canadian National Railways; CofG = Central of Georgia Railway; D&RGW = Denver & Rio Grande Western Railroad; IC = Illinois Central Railway; NdeM = National Railways of Mexico; N&W = Norfolk & Western Railway; P-S = Pullman-Standard Car Manufacturing Company; QNS&L = Quebec, North Shore & Labrador Railway; SCL = Seaboard Coast Line; SOU = Southern Railway; UP = Union Pacific Railroad; VIA = VIA

Atchison, Topeka & Santa Fe Railway

500		P-S 1950	*Super Chief*/Amtrak 9350
501		P-S 1950	*Super Chief*/Amtrak 9351
502		P-S 1950	*Super Chief*/Amtrak 9352
503		P-S 1950	*Super Chief*/Amtrak 9353
504		P-S 1950	*Super Chief*/Amtrak 9354
505		P-S 1950	*Super Chief*/Amtrak 9355
506		Budd 1954	*El Capitan, Chicagoan/ Kansas Cityan*
507		Budd 1954	*El Capitan, Chicagoan/ Kansas Cityan*/A-T 540
508		Budd 1954	*El Capitan, Chicagoan/ Kansas Cityan*/A-T 520
509		Budd 1954	*El Capitan, Chicagoan/ Kansas Cityan*/A-T 521
510		Budd 1954	*El Capitan, Chicagoan/ Kansas Cityan*/A-T 522
511		Budd 1954	*El Capitan, Chicagoan/ Kansas Cityan*/A-T 523
512		Budd 1954	*El Capitan, Chicagoan/ Kansas Cityan*/A-T 541
513		Budd 1954	*El Capitan, Chicagoan/ Kansas Cityan*/A-T 524
550		Budd 1954	*San Francisco Chief*/A-T 512
551		Budd 1954	*San Francisco Chief*/A-T 513
552		Budd 1954	*San Francisco Chief*/A-T 514
553		Budd 1954	*San Francisco Chief*/A-T 515
554		Budd 1954	*San Francisco Chief*/A-T 510
555		Budd 1954	*San Francisco Chief*/A-T 511

Baltimore & Ohio Railroad

5550	High Dome	P-S 1949	*Columbian*/Amtrak 9420
5551	Sky Dome	P-S 1949	*Columbian*/Amtrak 9421

Canadian Pacific Railway

500		Budd 1954	*Canadian/Dominion/* VIA 500, 8500
501		Budd 1954	*Canadian/Dominion/* VIA 501, 8501
502		Budd 1954	*Canadian/Dominion/* VIA 502, 8502
503		Budd 1954	*Canadian/Dominion/* VIA 503, 8503
504		Budd 1954	*Canadian/Dominion/* VIA 504, 8504
505		Budd 1954	*Canadian/Dominion/* VIA 505, 8505
506		Budd 1954	*Canadian/Dominion/* VIA 506, 8506
507		Budd 1954	*Canadian/Dominion/* VIA 507, 8507
508		Budd 1954	*Canadian/Dominion*/VIA 508
509		Budd 1954	*Canadian/Dominion/* VIA 509, 8509
510		Budd 1954	*Canadian/Dominion/* VIA 510, 8510
511		Budd 1954	*Canadian/Dominion/* VIA 511, 8511

Canadian Pacific Railway, continued

512		Budd 1954	*Canadian/Dominion/* VIA 512, 8512
513		Budd 1954	*Canadian/Dominion*/VIA 513
514		Budd 1954	*Canadian/Dominion/* VIA 514, 8514
515		Budd 1955	*Canadian/Dominion/* VIA 515, 8515
516		Budd 1955	*Canadian/Dominion/* VIA 516, 8516
517		Budd 1955	*Canadian/Dominion/* VIA 517, 8517
15401	Algonquin Park	Budd 1954	*Canadian/Dominion/* VIA 15401
15402	Assiniboine Park	Budd 1954	*Canadian/Dominion/* VIA 15402, 8702
15403	Banff Park	Budd 1954	*Canadian/Dominion/* VIA 15403, 8703
15404	Evangeline Park	Budd 1954	*Canadian/Dominion/* VIA 15404, 8704
15405	Fundy Park	Budd 1954	*Canadian/Dominion*
15406	Glacier Park	Budd 1954	*Canadian/Dominion/* VIA 15406, 8706
15407	Kokanee Park	Budd 1954	*Canadian/Dominion/* VIA 15407, 8707
15408	Kootenay Park	Budd 1954	*Canadian/Dominion/* VIA 15408, 8708
15409	Laurentide Park	Budd 1954	*Canadian/Dominion/* VIA 15409, 8709
15410	Prince Albert Park	Budd 1954	*Canadian/Dominion/* VIA 15410, 8710
15411	Revelstoke Park	Budd 1954	*Canadian/Dominion/* VIA 15411, 8711
15412	Riding Mtn. Park	Budd 1954	*Canadian/Dominion/* VIA 15412
15413	Sibley Park	Budd 1954	*Canadian/Dominion/* VIA 15413
15414	Strathcona Park	Budd 1954	*Canadian/Dominion/* VIA 15414, 8714
15415	Tremblant Park	Budd 1954	*Canadian/Dominion/* VIA 15415, 8715
15416	Tweedsmuir Park	Budd 1954	*Canadian/Dominion/* VIA 15416, 8716
15417	Waterton Park	QNS&L 1954	*Canadian/Dominion/* VIA 15417, 8717
15418	Yoho Park	Budd 1954	*Canadian/Dominion/* VIA 15418, 8718

Chesapeake & Ohio Railway

1850		Budd 1948	*Chessie*/B&O 7600 Moonlight Dome/ SCL 6800/ Amtrak 9200
1851		Budd 1948	*Chessie*/B&O 7601 Starlight Dome/ SCL 6801/Amtrak 9201
1852		Budd 1948	*Chessie*/B&O 7602 Sunlight Dome/ SCL 6802/Amtrak 9202

Chesapeake & Ohio Railway, continued

1875		Budd 1948	*Chessie*/D&RGW 1248
1876		Budd 1948	*Chessie*/D&RGW 1249/ Amtrak 9384
1877		Budd 1948	*Chessie*/D&RGW 1250

Chicago, Burlington & Quincy Railroad

235	Silver Chateau	Budd 1956	*Denver Zephyr*/Amtrak 9330
236	Silver Veranda	Budd 1956	*Denver Zephyr*/Amtrak 9331
250	Silver Club	Budd 1948	*California Zephyr*/ Amtrak 9810
251	Silver Lounge	Budd 1948	*California Zephyr*/ Amtrak 9811
252	Silver Roundup	Budd 1948	*California Zephyr*
253	Silver Cup	Budd 1956	*Denver Zephyr*/Amtrak 9813
254	Silver Kettle	Budd 1956	*Denver Zephyr*/ Amtrak 9814/VIA 8518
304		Budd 1954	*North Coast Limited*/ Amtrak 9225
305		Budd 1954	*North Coast Limited*/ Amtrak 9210
320	Silver Garden	Budd 1953	*Kansas City/American Royal Zephyrs*/ Amtrak 9800
321	Silver Patio	Budd 1953	*Kansas City/American Royal Zephyrs*/ Amtrak 9801/VIA 8523
360	Silver View	Budd 1947	*Twin Zephyrs*/Amtrak 9300
361	Silver Vista	Budd 1947	*Twin Zephyrs*/Amtrak 9301
365	Silver Terrace	Budd 1953	*Kansas City Zephyr*/ Amtrak 9320
366	Silver Tower	Budd 1953	*Kansas City Zephyr*/ Amtrak 9321
375	Silver Horizon	Budd 1948	*California Zephyr*/ Amtrak 9250
376	Silver Penthouse	Budd 1948	*California Zephyr*/ Amtrak 9251
377	Silver Solarium	Budd 1948	*California Zephyr*/ Amtrak 9252
378	Silver Lookout	Budd 1948	*California/Ak-Sar-Ben Zephyrs*/Amtrak 9253
557		Budd 1954	*North Coast Limited*/ Amtrak 9484
558		Budd 1954	*North Coast Limited*/ Amtrak 9485, 9406
1333		Budd 1955	*Empire Builder*/Amtrak 9473
1334		Budd 1955	*Empire Builder*/ Amtrak 9474/VIA 8521
1335		Budd 1955	*Empire Builder*/ Amtrak 9475, 9411
1395	River View	Budd 1955	*Empire Builder*/ Amtrak 9365, 9302
4709	Silver Castle	Budd 1940	Pool; rebuilt as dome/ Amtrak 9400
4714	Silver Alchemy	Budd 1940	Pool; rebuilt to Silver Dome/Amtrak 9401
4716	Silver Bridle	Budd 1948	*California Zephyr*/Amtrak 9450/ARR 7003
4717	Silver Lodge	Budd 1948	*California Zephyr*/Amtrak 9451/ARR 7005
4718	Silver Lariat	Budd 1948	*California Zephyr*/ Amtrak 9452
4719	Silver Ranch	Budd 1948	*California Zephyr*/ Amtrak 9453
4720	Silver Rifle	Budd 1948	*California Zephyr*/ Amtrak 9454
4721	Silver Saddle	Budd 1948	*California Zephyr*/ Amtrak 9455
4722	Silver Stirrup	Budd 1948	*California Zephyr*/ Amtrak 9456/ARR 7004
4723	Silver Bluff	Budd 1947	*Twin Zephyrs*/Amtrak 9500
4724	Silver Glade	Budd 1947	*Twin Zephyrs*/Amtrak 9501
4725	Silver Island	Budd 1947	*Twin Zephyrs*/Amtrak 9540
4726	Silver River	Budd 1947	*Twin Zephyrs*/ Amtrak 9541/VIA 8524

Chicago, Burlington & Quincy Railroad, continued

4727	Silver Stream	Budd 1947	*Twin Zephyrs*/Amtrak 9542
4728	Silver Wave	Budd 1947	*Twin Zephyrs*/Amtrak 954
4729	Silver Scene	Budd 1947	*Twin Zephyrs*/Amtrak 9544
4730	Silver Vision	Budd 1947	*Twin Zephyrs*/Amtrak 9545
4735	Silver Buckle	Budd 1956	*Denver Zephyr*/Amtrak 9457
4736	Silver Brand	Budd 1956	*Denver Zephyr*/Amtrak 9458

Chicago, Milwaukee, St. Paul & Pacific Railroad

50		P-S 1952	*Hiawathas*/CN 2400 *Jasper*/VIA 2700/ Amtrak 9310
51		P-S 1952	*Hiawathas*/CN 2404 *Qu'Appelle*/VIA 2704
52		P-S 1952	*Hiawathas*/CN 2405 *Columbia*/VIA 2705/ Amtrak 9311
53		P-S 1952	*Hiawathas*/CN 2401 *Athabaska*/VIA 2701
54		P-S 1952	*Hiawathas*/CN 2402 *Yellowhead*/VIA 2702
55		P-S 1952	*Hiawathas*/Amtrak 9380
56		P-S 1952	*Hiawathas*/CN 2403 *Fraser*/VIA 2703/ Amtrak 9312
57		P-S 1952	*Hiawathas*/Amtrak 9381
58		P-S 1952	*Hiawathas*/Amtrak 9382
59		P-S 1952	*Hiawathas*/Amtrak 9383

Denver & Rio Grande Western Railroad

1105	Silver Bronco	Budd 1948	*California Zephyr*
1106	Silver Colt	Budd 1948	*California Zephyr*/ Amtrak 9446/ARR 7022
1107	Silver Mustang	Budd 1948	*California Zephyr*/ Amtrak 9447/ARR 7011
1108	Silver Pony	Budd 1948	*California Zephyr*/ Amtrak 9448/ARR 7033
1140	Silver Shop	Budd 1948	*California Zephyr*/ VIA 8519
1145	Silver Sky	Budd 1949	*California Zephyr*/ VIA 15519 Jasper Park

General Motors

	Star Dust	P-S 1947	*Train of Tomorrow*/UP 7010
	Sky View	P-S 1947	*Train of Tomorrow*/UP 8010
	Moon Glow	P-S 1947	*Train of Tomorrow*/UP 9015
	Dream Cloud	P-S 1947	*Train of Tomorrow*/UP

Great Northern Railway

1320		Budd 1955	*Empire Builder*/Amtrak 9460
1321		Budd 1955	*Empire Builder*/Amtrak 9461
1322		Budd 1955	*Empire Builder*/Amtrak 9462
1323		Budd 1955	*Empire Builder*/Amtrak 9463
1324		Budd 1955	*Empire Builder*/Amtrak 9464
1325		Budd 1955	*Empire Builder*/ Amtrak 9465, 9409
1326		Budd 1955	*Empire Builder*/Amtrak 9466
1327		Budd 1955	*Empire Builder*/Amtrak 9467
1328		Budd 1955	*Empire Builder*/Amtrak 9468
1329		Budd 1955	*Empire Builder*/Amtrak 9469
1330		Budd 1955	*Empire Builder*/Amtrak 9470
1331		Budd 1955	*Empire Builder*/ Amtrak 9471, 9410
1390	Glacier View	Budd 1955	*Empire Builder*/Amtrak 9360
1391	Ocean View	Budd 1955	*Empire Builder*/ Amtrak 9361, 9300
1392	Mountain View	Budd 1955	*Empire Builder*/ Amtrak 9362, 9301
1393	Lake View	Budd 1955	*Empire Builder*/Amtrak 9363
1394	Prairie View	Budd 1955	*Empire Builder*/Amtrak 9364

International–Great Northern Railway

896		P-S 1952	*South/West Texas Eagles*/ IC 2211

Missouri Pacific Railroad

890	Budd 1948	*Colorado Eagle*/IC 2200/ CHP 521 *Ciudad de Chihuahua*
891	Budd 1948	*Colorado Eagle*/IC 2201
892	Budd 1948	*Colorado Eagle*/IC 2202
893	P-S 1952	*South/West Texas Eagles*
894	P-S 1952	*South/West Texas Eagles*/ IC 2210
895	P-S 1952	*South/West Texas Eagles*

Northern Pacific Railway

307	Budd 1954	*North Coast Limited*/ Amtrak 9220
308	Budd 1954	*North Coast Limited*/ Amtrak 9221
309	Budd 1954	*North Coast Limited*/ Amtrak 9212
310	Budd 1954	*North Coast Limited*/ Amtrak 9213
311	Budd 1954	*North Coast Limited*/ Amtrak 9222
312	Budd 1954	*North Coast Limited*/ Amtrak 9223
313	Budd 1954	*North Coast Limited*/ Amtrak 9214
314	Budd 1957	*North Coast Limited*/ Amtrak 9224
549	Budd 1957	*North Coast Limited*/ Amtrak 9476
550	Budd 1954	*North Coast Limited*/ Amtrak 9477, 9407
551	Budd 1954	*North Coast Limited*/ Amtrak 9478, 9400
552	Budd 1954	*North Coast Limited*/ Amtrak 9479, 9401
553	Budd 1954	*North Coast Limited*/ Amtrak 9480, 9402
554	Budd 1954	*North Coast Limited*/ Amtrak 9481, 9405
555	Budd 1954	*North Coast Limited*/ Amtrak 9482, 9403
556	Budd 1954	*North Coast Limited*/ Amtrak 9483, 9404

Southern Pacific

3600	SP 1954	*San Joaquin Daylight*
3601	SP 1955	*San Francisco Overland*/ Amtrak 9370
3602	SP 1955	*San Francisco Overland*/ Amtrak 9371
3603	SP 1955	*San Francisco Overland*/ Amtrak 9372
3604	SP 1955	*San Joaquin Daylight*/ Amtrak 9373
3605	SP 1955	*Shasta Daylight*/ Amtrak 9374
3606	SP 1955	*Shasta Daylight*

Spokane, Portland & Seattle Railway

306	Budd 1954	*North Coast Limited*/ Amtrak 9211
559	Budd 1954	*North Coast Limited*/ Amtrak 9486, 9408
1332	Budd 1955	*Empire Builder*/ Amtrak 9472/ ARR 7077/VIA 8520

Texas & Pacific Railway

200	P-S 1952	*South/West Texas Eagles*/ IC 2212

Union Pacific Railroad

7000	ACF 1954	*Challenger*/A-T 700
7001	ACF 1954	*Challenger*/A-T 701
7002	ACF 1954	*Challenger*/A-T 702
7003	ACF 1954	*Challenger*/A-T 703
7004	ACF 1954	*Challenger*/ARR 7004
7005	ACF 1954	*City of Portland*/A-T 704
7006	ACF 1954	*City of Portland*/NdeM 371
7007	ACF 1955	*City of Portland*/A-T 705
7008	ACF 1955	*City of Portland*/ARR 7008
7009	ACF 1955	*City of Portland*/A-T 706
7011	P-S 1958	*City of St. Louis*/A-T 707
7012	P-S 1958	*City of St. Louis*/A-T 708
7013	P-S 1958	*City of St. Louis*/ARR 7013
7014	P-S 1958	*City of St. Louis*/ARR 7014
7015	P-S 1958	*City of St. Louis*/A-T 709
8000	ACF 1955	*City of Los Angeles*/A-T 800
8001	ACF 1955	*City of Los Angeles*/A-T 801
8002	ACF 1955	*City of Los Angeles*/A-T 802
8003	ACF 1955	*City of Los Angeles*
8004	ACF 1955	*City of Los Angeles*/A-T 803
8005	ACF 1955	*City of Portland*/A-T 804
8006	ACF 1955	*City of Portland*/A-T 805
8007	ACF 1955	*City of Portland*/A-T 806
8008	ACF 1955	*City of Portland*/A-T 807
8009	ACF 1955	*City of Portland*/A-T 808
9000	ACF 1955	*City of Los Angeles*/A-T 900
9001	ACF 1955	*City of Los Angeles*/A-T 901
9002	ACF 1955	*City of Los Angeles*/A-T 902
9003	ACF 1955	*City of Los Angeles*/A-T 903
9004	ACF 1955	*City of Los Angeles*
9005	ACF 1955	*City of Portland*/A-T 904
9006	ACF 1955	*City of Portland*/A-T 905
9007	ACF 1955	*City of Portland*/A-T 542
9008	ACF 1955	*City of Portland*/A-T 907
9009	ACF 1955	*City of Portland*/A-T 908
9010	ACF 1955	*City of St. Louis*/A-T 909
9011	ACF 1955	*City of St. Louis*/A-T 543
9012	ACF 1955	*City of St. Louis*/A-T 911
9013	ACF 1955	*City of St. Louis*/A-T 912
9014	ACF 1955	*City of St. Louis*/A-T 913

Wabash

200	Budd 1950	*Blue Bird*/Amtrak 9560
201	Budd 1950	*Blue Bird*/Amtrak 9561
202	Budd 1950	*Blue Bird*/Amtrak 9562
203	P-S 1958	*City of St. Louis*/ CofG 1613/ SOU 1613/ QNS&L 13510
1601	Budd 1950	*Blue Bird*/Amtrak 9310
1602	P-S 1952	*Blue Bird*/CofG 1602/ SOU 1602

Western Pacific Railroad

811	Silver Dollar	Budd 1948	*California Zephyr*/A-T 460
812	Silver Feather	Budd 1948	*California Zephyr*/A-T 461
813	Silver Palace	Budd 1948	*California Zephyr*/A-T 462
814	Silver Sage	Budd 1948	*California Zephyr*/A-T 463
815	Silver Schooner	Budd 1948	*California Zephyr*/A-T 470
816	Silver Scout	Budd 1948	*California Zephyr*/A-T 471
817	Silver Thistle	Budd 1948	*California Zephyr*/ A-T 464/VIA 8522
831	Silver Chalet	Budd 1948	*California Zephyr*/ CB&Q second 252/ Amtrak 9812
832	Silver Hostel	Budd 1948	*California Zephyr*/ D&RGW 832
881	Silver Crescent	Budd 1948	*California Zephyr*
882	Silver Planet	Budd 1948	*California Zephyr*

Bibliography

Benson, Ted and MacGregor, Bruce. *Portrait of a Silver Lady*. Boulder, Colo.: Pruett Publishing Company, 1977.

Davis, Michael B. "Prospector — The Judge's Train," *Colorado Rail Annual Number Nine*. Golden, Colo.: Colorado Railroad Museum, 1971.

Dorin, Patrick C. *The Domeliners*. Seattle: Superior Publishing Company, 1973.

Dubin, Arthur D. *More Classic Trains*. Milwaukee: Kalmbach Publishing Co., 1974.

Dubin, Arthur D. *Some Classic Trains*. Milwaukee: Kalmbach Publishing Co., 1964.

Edmonson, Harold A. *Journey to Amtrak*. Milwaukee: Kalmbach Publishing Co., 1972.

Farrington, S. Kip Jr. *Railroading the Modern Way*. New York: Coward-McCann, 1951.

Farrington, S. Kip Jr. *Railroads of the Hour*. New York: Coward-McCann, 1958.

Frailey, Fred W. *Zephyrs, Chiefs, and Other Orphans*. Godfrey, Ill.: RPC Publications, 1977.

Glischinski, Steve. "Going Out (and Back) for Dinner," *Trains* magazine, L (June 1990), 26–35.

Mertens, Maurice. *Les Trans Europ Express*. Paris: La Vie du Rail, 1985.

Norwood, John M. *Rio Grande Memories*. Forest Park, Ill.: Heimburger House Publishing Company, 1991.

Overton, Richard C. *Burlington Route*. New York: Alfred A. Knopf, 1965.

Perl, Anthony. "Alaska Domeliners," International Railway Traveler (November/December, 1990), 10–13.

Randall, W. David. *Railway Passenger Car Annual, Volume V*. Godfrey, Ill.: RPC Publications, 1984.

Ranks, Harold E. and Kratville, William W. *Union Pacific Streamliners*. Omaha: Kratville Publications, 1974

Reck, Franklin M. *On Time*. Electro-Motive Division, 1948.

Schafer, Mike. *All Aboard Amtrak*. Piscataway, N.J.: Railpace Company, 1991.

Scribbins, Jim. *The Hiawatha Story*. Milwaukee: Kalmbach Publishing Co., 1970.

Wayner, Robert J. *Amtrak Car and Locomotive Spotter* (various editions). New York: Wayner Publications, 1972, 1976, 1980.

Wayner, Robert J. *Car Names, Numbers, and Consists*. New York: Wayner Publications, 1972.

Welsh, Joe. "Rarest of the Rare," *Passenger Train Journal*, XXII (September 1991), 26–29.

Welsh, Joe. "Seaboard's Sun Lounge Sleepers," *Passenger Train Journal*, XIX (November 1988), 24–28.

White, John H. *The American Railroad Passenger Car*. Baltimore: The Johns Hopkins University Press, 1978.

The Official Guide of the Railways (various issues). New York: National Railway Publication Company.

Railway Age (various issues)

Trains magazine (various issues)